THEOCRACY

IN PAUL'S PRAXIS
AND THEOLOGY

D1002670

THEOCRACY

IN PAUL'S PRAXIS
AND THEOLOGY

Dieter Georgi

translated by David E. Green

Fortress Press   Minneapolis

THEOCRACY IN PAUL'S PRAXIS AND THEOLOGY

Translated from the German, "Gott auf den Kopf stellen," in Jacob Taubes, ed., *Theokratie* (Paderborn: Ferdinand Schöningh, 1987).

Scripture quotations unless otherwise noted are from the Revised Standard Version of the Bible, copyright © 1946, 1952, and 1971 by the Division of Christian Education of the National Council of Churches.

Interior and cover design: Carol Evans-Smith

Library of Congress Cataloging-in-Publication Data
Georgi, Dieter,
    [Gott auf den Kopf stellen. English]
    Theocracy in Paul's praxis and theology / by Dieter Georgi : translated by David E. Green.
      p.   cm.
    Translation of: Gott auf den Kopf stellen.
    Includes bibliographical references and index.
    ISBN 0-8006-2468-8
    1. Bible.   N.T.   Epistles of Paul—Criticism, interpretation, etc.
    2. Theocracy—Biblical teaching.   3. Theocracy—History of doctrines—Early church, ca. 30-600.   I. Title.
    BS2651.G46   1991
    227'.06—dc20   91-6581
                                            CIP

The paper used in this publication meets the minimum requirements of American National Standard for Information Sciences—Permanence of Paper for Printed Library Materials, ANSI Z329.48-1984. ∞™

Manufactured in the U.S.A.   AF 1-2468

95   94   93   92   91   1   2   3   4   5   6   7   8   9   10

CONTENTS

PREFACE

Having taught for fifteen years at Harvard Divinity School, I was intrigued, when I later became dean of a divinity school at a large German state university, to meet in the academic senate with deans of other schools and to recognize them too as "divinity schools" in disguise. Religious and theological issues of the past have now been submerged into the presuppositions of most of our scholarly disciplines, even the natural sciences. A major task of critical scholarly discourse today is uncovering such hidden, unquestioned, but all the more virulent premises in their secular camouflage.

The German version of the following study was an element of such discussion on the interplay of theology and other sciences. It consisted originally of a series of theses that then were enlarged into an essay published by Jacob Taubes with the other papers. He had organized three conferences, each of them at the Reimers foundation in Bad Homburg, Germany. The aegis for all three meetings was the theory of religion and political theology. The first conference was on the German political scientist Carl Schmitt, the second on Gnosticism and politics, and the third on theocracy.[1] I contributed to the second and third conferences.

During the conference on theocracy and in the subsequent volume of papers and essays, it became apparent that the concept of theocracy remains active, though usually not appearing in the literal form of that term. It has disguised itself rather well in most cases. My own essay therefore has not only a historical-critical side. Contemporary theological, social, and political issues are at stake as well. My focus is most

---

1. See *Religions-theorie und politische Theologie,* ed. Jacob Taubes, vol. 3: *Theokratie* (Paderborn: Ferdinand Schöningh, 1987).

of all on a certain variant of the biblical-theological heritage regarding God's rule: the concept of sovereignty.

Sovereignty appears as a matter of course in today's political science and practice. But it is relatively new in the world of politics. It was first used as an explicitly political and legal term by the former Carmelite monk and theologian (and later historical critic, economist, jurist, public prosecutor and persecutor of witches, then bourgeois deputy to the estates general of Blois), Jean Bodin (1529–96).[2] The concept initially described superior authority on whatever feudal level, from king down to husband. It had come to a more common use in the late fourteenth and fifteenth centuries.

As the term denoted preeminence and controlling power, sovereignty consciously mirrored divine majesty and supremacy. Application of the concept to human authorities—most of all to the real power figures, the royal "sovereigns"—and its emphasis on independence and supreme controlling force recall the medieval understanding of the divine *majestas,* more precisely the *aseitas* or aseity of God. God for these medieval theologians is the utmost autocrat, the highest and underived authority, the ultimate self. God is independent and self-sufficient, the unchallengable number one, the only one entitled to and able to generate self-definition. God does not owe anything to anyone. This tendency toward considering God as *causa sui,* the only self-cause, and thus independent and absolute source of God's own will, power, and potential, gained the upper hand in the debate between realists and nominalists over this matter. The medieval deity is a law unto itself, and its power is limited only by God's self. Natural law is this deity's basic law.

Such thinking about God's absolute sovereignty reflects not biblical notions but Hellenistic philosophy of divine and

2. Jean Bodin, *The Response of Jean Bodin to the Paradoxes of Malestroit,* trans. G. A. Moore (Washington, 1946); idem, *The Six Books of a Commonweale,* new ed. K. D. MacRae (Cambridge, Mass., 1962); idem, *De la Démonomanie des Sorciers,* Paris, 1580 (German translation, *Vom ausgelasnen wütigen Teufelsheer,* by J. Fischart of 1581, 3d ed., Strasburg, 1591; reprinted by Graz, 1973).

human rulership. Another essential element from Hellenistic philosophy also appearing in the medieval concept of God's absolute authority is the notion of God's philanthropy, God's love for humans. Here the relationship to the biblical understanding of love is only secondary.[3]

God's majesty was a key term in Bodin's description of sovereignty in the political and legal realm. The independence of the state's power and its incorporation of legal authority, beneficial to the reasonable and merciless toward the irrational and demonic, reads easily as a complete translation of medieval ideas about God's aseity into the context of human societies and their governing authorities. Bodin was an advocate of reason, but this reason is bound up with economical effectiveness, reflecting God's creativity. Reproduction is basic for this social and economic productivity, which mirrors divine activity here on earth. Anything that interferes with reasonable reproduction and thus with productivity—the activity of witches, for instance—corrupts God's basic economy and is therefore demonic. Such corrupting and objectionable machinations need to be uncovered and extinguished. Sovereignty in fact is literally de*fined,* described from the *finis* or outside limit, not from its inner core. Without first and foremost setting limits and establishing borders that determine "out" and foe, this sovereignty (and its concomitant deity) would not know of "in" or of friend. Thus Bodin's intellectual and physical witch-hunting was not an atavism but part of his modern theory of state, as was his twentieth-century disciple Carl Schmitt's flirtation with fascism.[4]

3. Hellenistic rulers and their gods were conceived as benefactors, and philanthropy is in Hellenistic understanding a basic element of authentic rule (see the two articles in *Pauly-Wissowa, TRE* on "Philanthropos" by Johann Schmidt, 19,2: col. 2125, and on "Philanthropon" by Heinz Kortenbeutel, ibid., Suppl. 7: 1032–1034). Understanding God as absolute ruler is not antithetical to this but essentially concomitant. Nor is it in contradiction to the evolution of the medieval and early modern *bourgeoisie* and its individualism, but a natural accompaniment of it. On this evolution and its relation to a certain understanding of the figure of Jesus and of God's reign, see my article on "Leben-Jesu-Theologie/Leben-Jesu-Forschung" in *TRE,* vol. 20, forthcoming.

4. Bodin's theory is not only theological, legal, and political, but also economic,

The rather different deliberations of Paul open new vistas on sovereignty in the political and legal sphere. Paul's concepts of law and justification, both intimately related to his Christology, find little echo in political science or political debates today, which remain dominated by the camouflaged theology of sovereignty.

I wonder whether the emphasis in recent decades on the divinity of God as an absolute value is no more than a rediscovery of the medieval understanding of God. I wonder also whether Bodin, who had relations to the Huguenots, is not the real godfather of this theological passion. Its fierceness and exclusivity have much in common with Bodin's description of the concept of sovereignty—but without the idea of natural law, and therefore without any boundaries or limitations.

I write these lines during the two days in which Germany is being reunited, receiving back its full "sovereignty" and holding the first session of the all-German parliament. Sovereignty here appears as a takeover of a peaceful revolution of the people by political professionals of another system with a strong economy, and all of this by persons who profess to

---

including a well-developed monetary conception, presented first in Bodin's *The Response*. Adam Smith's *An Inquiry into the Nature and Causes of the Wealth of Nations* (1776; new edition by Edwin R. A. Seligman, London: Dent, 1910; New York: Everyman's Library, 1960), shows dependence on Bodin in many ways, particularly by entitling the last chapter of his book, "Of the Revenue of the Sovereign or Commonwealth." There Smith differentiates his discussion of "the Expenses of the Sovereign or Commonwealth" into "the Expense of Defense," "the Expense of Justice," and "the Expense of Public Works and Public Institutions." Armor was and is the first and main sign of sovereignty. Social obligations of the politically and legally constituted society remain last as well as least, if of political and legal interest at all. The belief that the concept of the free market would tend to preclude a strong, higly armed state is to this day a delusion. See also my discussion of some Pauline perspectives on money and economics and their contemporary relevance in my forthcoming book, *Remembering the Poor* (Decatur, Georgia: Abingdon, 1991). Neither Bodin nor Smith excludes the democratic form of authority and state from their understanding of sovereignty and its political, legal, and economic application; they include it. The real-socialist and the bourgeois-capitalist concepts of democracy had one idea in common, that of a heavily armed state; *wehrhafte Demokratie* is the magic word in German. And now after the demise of "real-socialism"?

be Christians! Is that what Christianity has to offer to the political world today? My study raises some fundamental biblical questions about that kind of Christian politics, practiced in the name of sovereignty.

My thanks go to the translator, David Green, and to Harold Rast, Michael West, the late John Hollar, Marshall Johnson, and the other people of Fortress Press for their excellent work and support. Kelly Del Tredici also deserves my gratitude for her assistance in giving the work its final polish.

I dedicate this study to my old friend and colleague, James Luther Adams, whose liberal thinking has been and remains a hearty stimulation for me.

Frankfurt/Main   —*Dieter Georgi*
October 4, 1990

1

THEOCRACY IN ISRAEL

"THERE IS NO GOD BUT ONE," Paul says in 1 Cor. 8:4 (cf. Gal. 3:20; Rom. 3:30). These words voice his continuity with Jewish tradition, which is based on Deut. 6:4: "Hear, O Israel: The Lord is our God, the Lord alone." For Paul, God is not only the almighty Lord of creation (Rom. 1:20; 4:17; 11:36) but also the Lord of history and humanity, as Romans 9 makes abundantly clear with a wealth of biblical examples.

From the very outset, the description of the biblical God as unique and omnipotent had a political dimension, which it never lost. As it enshrined the religious experiences of individuals and groups, so also it reflected political models and implied political demands.

These ideas motivated the loyalty of the Israelite people, establishing the authority of their social identity and system of government. They brought Israel's political institutions into being and enabled them to prevail. Israel's conflict with the world around it was not only religious but also social and political. The conflict was reflected in Israel's way of life as well as in its understanding of God. Foreign elements, too, found their way into Israel's own faith in both theory and praxis in the course of this critical dialogue.

These observations are already obvious for the period before the exile. They are illustrated clearly by the intimate bond between covenant, people, and cult, not to mention the analogy between divine and human monarchy and the relationship of both to the royal cult.[1]

After the fall of the monarchy, however, exilic and post-exilic Israel had to concentrate even more on a concrete—and therefore political—understanding of God in order to define and preserve its own identity. The priestly source (P) accomplishes this by radically separating the priesthood and cult from the embrace of the monarchy and focusing instead on the law as the dominant force in Israel. In P, the concepts of God's creative power and God's rule over the world stand in inverse relationship to Israel's loss of independence and the destruction of its institutions, including the temple, which was destroyed and had not yet been rebuilt when P was writing. P's portrayal of Israel's period of wandering in the desert echoes the life in exile shared by the author and the leading priestly classes.

Notions about God and the cult developed by Ezekiel are also linked inextricably to socio-political situations, ideas, and plans growing out of the exile and its forced separation of the upper classes from the lower classes who were left behind. The reforms of Nehemiah and Ezra were likewise basically aristocratic and cultic, being carried out under the authority of the foreign Persian regime. The institution of a vassal temple state was familiar in a variety of forms throughout the Mediterranean world, particularly in the Near East. Its

1. The articles by Frank M. Cross in his *Canaanite Myth and Hebrew Epic* (Cambridge: Harvard University Press, 1973) provide an excellent insight into this world. In the course of history, these social and political elements became increasingly problematic: protest movements led to alternative systems and institutions. This development does not disprove the political implications but rather confirms their significance. They were modified but never eliminated. Yet the history of biblical interpretation has seen repeated attempts to claim that the Bible—in whole or in part—is concerned solely with religious or personal matters. This is particularly true of the New Testament. Critical analysis of such "spiritualizing" interpretations shows that they, too, all invariably serve substantial political interests.

self-imposed restriction to a small ethnic and religious community was clearly consonant with the interests of Persia, which was not seeking internationally minded adherents of universalistic Yahwism. The reader of Ezra and Nehemiah is struck by the mixture of Israelite and Persian terms for God— an especially interesting observation in the light of the reformers' concern for cultic and ethnic purity. Syncretism and purism thus seem no more irreconcilable than confession of the sovereignty of God alone and acceptance of the sovereignty of a foreign power adhering to a different religion.

The Wisdom Movement

It would be wrong to assume that the postexilic period produced a Jewish understanding of religion and society that was unique and homogeneous, with a similarly homogenous concept of God. On the contrary. One element not yet mentioned, the Jewish wisdom movement, was to be very important for the future. It was especially important for the Jesus movement, including Paul. The wisdom movement was itself a complex phenomenon with internal tensions and conflicts. It was extensively concerned with socio-political questions, and exhibited a critical attitude toward other Israelite and Jewish traditions and institutions.[2]

Above all, it repeatedly challenged various claims of certain institutions to represent the power of God in the world and therefore also in Israel.[3]

Theological wisdom (Proverbs 1–10, echoed with overtones of parody in the speeches of Job's three friends, and

2. See Dieter Georgi, "Das Wesen der Weisheit nach der Weisheit Salomos," in *Gnosis und Politik*, ed. Jacob Taubes (Paderborn: Schöningh, 1984), 66–81, 90–91.

3. This holds true already for preexilic Israelite experiential wisdom, which even today causes difficulty for scholars trying to assign it a niche in society. In my opinion, this earliest branch of the Jewish wisdom movement was not entirely conformist.

reflecting the charismatic wisdom that will be discussed later) had ceased to put any stock in institutions of an earlier age: king or temple, cult or priesthood. Such statements as Prov. 3:9-10 show that this form of wisdom was familiar with the cult. Even the long thirty-first chapter of Job, which is probably secondary and already betrays the influence of skeptical wisdom, presupposes and imitates the oath of purgation from the Israelite cult. This makes the otherwise total silence of theological wisdom concerning the cult all the more astonishing. In view of the importance of the cult in the reflections of other exilic and postexilic circles, I am compelled to interpret this silence as criticism: for wisdom, the cult was not central but incidental—a notion that Ezekiel, P, Nehemiah, and Ezra would have cursed.

The theories and claims of the exiles interested in cultic reform and restoration and of their later postexilic disciples did not impress the representatives of theological wisdom. They rather thought in terms of an immediate, assured presence of God and of God's wisdom, personally accessible and effective. Wisdom can be experienced as "sister" and "intimate friend" (Prov. 7:4); she can be "sought" and "searched for" (2:4), or "gained" (4:7), for she is like a woman crying in the street (1:20-23) or a loved one upon her bed (7–9, in contrast to the harlot folly). Wisdom promises and bestows what Deut. 30:10-20 says of the "word of God" and the "law of the Lord." Wisdom is clearer and more rational than cultic ordinances. This is the primary theme of Proverbs 8, especially vv. 8-11. For Jews who came increasingly in contact with Gentiles, it was significant that wisdom was understood as embracing the entire realm of creation and nature (Prov. 3:19) and serving all kings and governors (8:15-16).

Exilic and postexilic theological wisdom shared a fundamentally optimistic attitude with the practical wisdom of the preexilic period. But theological wisdom, as it responded to the catastrophe of the exile, could no longer focus only on the experiences of individuals and groups. Like Greek philosophy of the same period, theological wisdom tried instead to conjure up a unified world that might be glimpsed behind the multiplicity of the world of experience. This unified world was reflected in nature and known through wisdom (see especially Proverbs 8). Beyond specific ethnic groups and their specific institutions, a universal consciousness could be observed in human behavior. This element could not be contained within any local or provincial shell. It was not only native Judahites who disagreed with the "reforms" of the two Judeo-Persian officials. There were also a growing number of Jews who dwelt or traveled outside the temple state of Ezra and Nehemiah, who found helpful guidelines in what this "theological wisdom" had to offer.[4]

The optimism embodied in this movement did not, however, hold up to the critical observations of experience. Skeptical wisdom (Ecclesiastes, the words of Agur in Proverbs 30, and the speeches of Job, especially Job 28) meditated increasingly on the vicissitudes of human experience and history. It questioned the presence and accessibility of wisdom or intelligible divine power in nature and even in history. The refrain that all is vanity and that the ways of God are remote and incomprehensible pervades Ecclesiastes. Job 28 describes the *absence* of wisdom: it is utterly inaccessible (see also Prov. 30:3-4). The circles which voiced such views probably belonged to the upper strata of society. The soberness expressed in this skepticism was averse to all forms of speculation, mysticism, and magic. It looked for God's presence and divine wisdom exclusively in the here and now of daily life (see Eccl. 5:17 [Eng. v. 28]).

At the end of the third century B.C.E., political revolution, in all likelihood coupled with economic prosperity, brought about an astonishing increase in the power of the Jerusalem priesthood, culminating in the person of the High Priest Simon the Just. His constructive program is reflected above all in

4. Whether this theological wisdom led to the formation of schools and a school tradition is disputed. In my opinion, the tendency toward inclusive forms and universal ideas argues in favor of such a development. This tendency differs sharply from the experiential wisdom in the second part of Proverbs—with the exception of chap. 30.

6 Theocracy in Paul

the book of his protégé Jesus ben Sirach, to whom he entrusted the task of interpreting the law as a clear system of popular morality. He also entrusted him to develop a school of sages who were to educate the people.[5]

In a culture devoted to the extraordinary and abounding in miracles,[6] the charismatic wisdom of Jesus ben Sirach interpreted the law as the incorporation of Lady Wisdom, the very essence of the miraculous. Law was the author and heart of creation and its moral order, miraculously present in Israel and its Jerusalem-based temple cult. Because of this, it radiated outward into the scribal academies. In ben Sirach's day, Israel faced the beguiling but threatening claims of the new Hellenistic civilization with its impressive bureaucracy and technology, its pervasive educational and economic system. Charismatic wisdom bore witness that Israel's Torah enshrined the order—not merely of Israel but of the entire world, including the pagan civilization that claimed to be so wonderous. The scribes, the interpreters of Torah, had direct access to the heart of all matters, the constitution of the world, of history, of society, of civilization, of every individual. They and the temple priests of Jerusalem were therefore the real miracle workers. Through the law, they had access also to the constitutive power behind the law, the sovereign power of God. This power was revealed in the Torah, and it represented the metaphysical and moral order which actively governed and controlled the world.

5. It is hard to say whether Jesus Sirach himself already had colleagues and whether the class of sages he was to develop as a group of "scribes" was already in existence (at least in the third century); but both assumptions are likely.
6. See Dieter Georgi, "Socioeconomic Reasons for the 'Divine Man' as a Propagandistic Pattern," in *Aspects of Religious Propaganda in Judaism and Early Christianity*, ed. Elisabeth Schüssler Fiorenza (Notre Dame: University of Notre Dame Press, 1967), 29–42. See also the epilogue in Dieter Georgi, *The Opponents of Paul in Second Corinthians* (Philadelphia: Fortress Press, 1986), 333–450, esp. 390–422. For the original German edition (minus the epilogue), see *Die Gegner des Paulus im 2. Korintherbrief: Studien zur religiösen Propoganda in der Spätantike,* WMANT 11 (Neukirchen: Neukirchener Verlag, 1964).

Jewish Apocalyptic, Missionary Theology, and Gnosticism

The New Testament writers (particularly Paul) were influenced primarily by the three later branches of the Jewish wisdom movement: apocalypticism, Jewish missionary theology, and Gnosticism.[7] Scholars generally acknowledge Paul's debt to Jewish apocalypticism.[8] But texts like 2 Cor. 4:17-18 and Romans 15 also contain clear echoes of pagan eschatology. It is hard to say whether Paul had direct access to such eschatological thinking or came to it by way of the Hellenistic synagogue, which was quite open to dialogue with its environment. But many non-Jewish ideas clearly came to Paul through the syncretistic nature of all three later forms of the wisdom movement. Not least among these ideas was the political philosophy of Hellenism, which Paul also knew in its Romanized form.[9]

Apocalypticism revived the theological and political ideas associated with the primal myth of a fundamental struggle

7. For a discussion of these three phenomena, see Georgi, "Wesen der Weisheit," 66–73.

8. See most recently J. Christiaan Beker, *Paul, the Apostle: The Triumph of God in Life and Thought* (Philadelphia: Fortress Press, 1980), esp. 135–181; and idem, *Paul's Apocalyptic Gospel: The Coming Triumph of God* (Philadelphia: Fortress Press, 1982). Beker, however, stresses this influence at the expense of the other religious movements mentioned above. Comparison of the fragments of 2 Corinthians with 1 Corinthians reveals the much greater range of Paul's thinking.

9. The Wisdom of Solomon, which represents an earlier form of the wisdom traditions used by Paul, illustrates how the Hellenistic kingship ideology found widespread (albeit critical) acceptance. See Dieter Georgi, "Weisheit Salomos," in *Jüdische Schriften aus hellenistisch-römischer Zeit*, ed. Werner Georg Kümmel (Gütersloh: Mohn, 1980), vol. 3, part 4, pp. 389–478. Some years ago, Erwin Goodenough demonstrated this influence on the religious philosophy of Philo of Alexandria, especially in his *By Light, Light: The Mystic Gospel of Hellenistic Judaism* (New Haven: Yale University Press, 1935), based on idem, "The Political Philosophy of Hellenistic Kingship," *Yale Classical Studies* 1 (1928): 53–102. Also important is James M. Reese, *Hellenistic Influence on the Book of Wisdom and Its Consequences*, Analecta Biblica 41 (Rome: Biblical Institute Press, 1980).

between God and a divine rebel. This myth, found also in the pagan world, had played an important role in preexilic Israel—particularly in the monarchic tradition and the royal ritual. In this myth and the societies associated with it, creation was the (re)assertion and the (re)establishment of order against chaos. The dominant institutions and their laws—invariably patriarchal—considered themselves representatives and defenders of an order that had been rescued miraculously from the forces of chaos; they needed constantly to defend this order against these forces. The preexilic scripture prophets—probably because they were consistently hostile to the monarchy—had traditionally either avoided this motif or reshaped it into a pacifistic protest against the monarchy. (Prophets loyal to the monarchy most likely did not follow this course.) The fall of the monarchy made it possible for the exilic and postexilic *epigoni* of these prophets to use the myth of the holy war without reservation.[10]

The apocalypse of Daniel and subsequent apocalyptic literature adopted the motif of the holy war from the prophets and gave it an even more radical twist, clearly using it as a weapon of political criticism. Instead of securing the foundations of the monarchy, this motif became a vehicle of protest against Antiochus IV, the Maccabeans, the Hasmoneans, and finally Herod and his family as well as the Roman leaders. Apocalypticism turned kings and rulers of every stripe into villains, the primary representatives of evil on this earth. This held true also for the Essenes who specifically attacked the high priests of Jerusalem and their political power.[11]

Under the influence of apocalypticism, the myth of the holy war, of a divine conflict, came to represent God as a king

10. On the importance of this myth for exilic and above all postexilic prophecy, see Paul D. Hanson, *The Dawn of Apocalyptic* (Philadelphia: Fortress Press, 1975).

11. Contrary to the political ideology and practice of modern Christian apocalypticism, the community of Qumran-believers will not actively participate in the rather dramatic divine battle of the endtime, so the Qumran War-Scroll emphasizes. The believers will merely engage in cheerleading performances like flag-waving, singing, praying, and watching. As everywhere else in Apocalyptic Wisdom, the divine army is of supernatural nature. Active human interference would be blasphemous.

triumphant over the chaos of the first and last days: in the end, God would be the sole ruler. Was this synonymous with the notion of absolute monarchy? Did the ideas associated with a heavenly book in which all was written anticipate Orwell's nightmare of 1984? Was the apocalyptic deity "big brother"? One can hear echoes of this notion in some apocalypses. Moreover, the Christian idea of God, especially after the political victory of Christianity, undoubtedly continued to elaborate this picture while it failed to notice the universal apocalyptic protest against all earthly power.

Above all, people overlooked (as they still do) the clear democratizing purpose of the apocalypse of Daniel. Here the vision of the heavenly son of man in Daniel 7 plays a key role.[12] Initially, the son of man is described as a preexistent heavenly figure (Dan. 7:13) to whom judgment and dominion are given (7:14). In 7:22, the heavenly individual is reinterpreted as referring to angels—this shift probably antedated the apocalypse of Daniel. Next the author of the present apocalypse modified this interpretation. Now (7:27) the heavenly "son of man" represents "the people of the saints of the Most High"—clearly human figures, the just of the eschaton and above all the apocalyptic martyrs (see 7:25). "Their kingdom shall be an everlasting kingdom, and all dominions shall serve and obey them" (7:27b). At the end of chapter seven the text does not even speak of God. These apocalyptic martyrs, "those who are wise," appear again in 12:3, in conjunction with motifs suggesting exaltation to the heavens: "Those who are wise shall shine like the brightness of the firmament; and those who turn many to righteousness, like the stars for ever and ever." It is a matter of debate whether this passage implies exaltation in rank as well as ascension.[13] Nickelsburg has

12. In the following discussion, I draw on Elliot Mvuyiswa Khoza Mgojo, "The Democratization of the Royal Ideology in the New Testament and Related Literature" (Ph.D. diss., Harvard University, 1975).

13. In favor of this interpretation, see George Nickelsburg, *Resurrection, Immortality, and Eternal Life in Intertestamental Judaism*, Harvard Theological Studies 26 (Cambridge: Harvard University Press, 1972), 82. I do not find the evidence so

pointed out[14] that Dan. 12:3 interprets Isaiah 52–53 (the song of the Suffering Servant), and in so doing multiplies this divine agent.[15]

Apocalyptic literature provides other examples of democratizing multiplication of hierarchical and monarchic roles, especially of the royal office. The future rule of the righteous over the unrighteous is predicted by 1 Enoch 96:1 (see also 92:4). In the eschatological future, according to 1 Enoch 108:11, God not only will surround the righteous with heavenly light—i.e., clothe them with (divine) glory—but also will set all of them on thrones, thereby raising them at least to the rank of vassal kings.

The similitudes of Enoch (1 Enoch 37–71) in particular continue to democratize the figure of the Son of Man.[16] The terms "elect" and "righteous" clearly are used both in the singular, as titles for the Son of Man, and in the plural, as attributes of the faithful. The two usages are closely intertwined; at the very beginning for instance, one finds "when the congregation of the righteous will be seen" (38:1) as well as "when the righteous one appears before the righteous" (38:2). The same verse adds "When light breaks forth for those who are righteous and elect upon the earth." Whatever the conclusions of source and tradition criticism, the exaltation of Enoch as son of man in 1 Enoch 71 is not alien to the similitudes. Rather it points out the correlation: the Son of Man has become a corporate figure, Enoch a paradigmatic

---

persuasive. The "brightness" is clearly the glory of the heavens; Nickelsburg himself (ibid., 60 n. 37) has pointed out the correlation between stars and angels. Mgojo ("Democratization," 44) sees here democratizing language borrowed from Trito-Isaiah (Isa. 62:3). The democratizing program of Isaiah 60–62 is discussed by Hanson, *Dawn*, 67–69.

14. Nickelsburg, *Resurrection*, 24–26.

15. Of course this development builds on the collective interpretation of the figure in the context of the Servant Songs.

16. In the following discussion, I have drawn especially on Nils Astrup Dahl, *Das Volk Gottes: Eine Untersuchung zum Kirchenbewusstsein des Urchristentums* (Darmstadt: Wissenschaftliche Buchgesellschaft, 1963), 84–91.

figure. The exaltation of the son of man as eschatological judge and ruler is the corporate future of all the righteous.[17]

The Wisdom of Solomon provides evidence that this apocalyptic treatment of tradition in like manner marks the beginning of Gnostic wisdom. I have discussed elsewhere[18] the transfer of the apocalyptic protest into this document. It brings together the apocalyptic traditions of divine conflict, exaltation and ascension, and a multiplication of both the figures of Enoch and of the suffering servant of Isaiah 52–53. In my annotated translation of the Wisdom of Solomon,[19] I have expanded on Reese's theory that this biblical document presupposes and incorporates the Hellenistic kingship philosophy. It does so, however, critically: the wise, not the reigning kings and rulers, are the true rulers. Wisd. of Sol. 6 illustrates the apocalyptic protest against earthly rulers, who can be rescued only by conversion to the character and calling of the wise. These sages are brought not only within the embrace of heavenly wisdom but also within the embrace of God. Just as "wisdom" can stand for "God" and "God" for "wisdom," so too the "wise" can represent "wisdom" or even "God"—most clearly in 5:1-13, where the parousia of the wise is the parousia of the divine judge of the world. This notion marks a radical change in the structures of authority associated with the faith of Israel.

The development of these themes could be traced further in Joseph and Aseneth, an elaborate allegorical narrative, which, in my opinion, belongs to this same branch of nascent Jewish Gnosticism. Joseph appears throughout as king and son of God—the latter in the sense of God's authorized representative. The text says little about God's own activity. In

17. Much could be added here about the tradition of the heavenly chariot throne and the related notions of ascension and exaltation. Although the development of these ideas would help us understand not only the religious but also the political ideology of Judaism and Christianity, the complexity of the material precludes such a presentation here.

18. Georgi, "Wesen der Weisheit," 71–78.

19. See n. 9 above.

this allegory Aseneth represents not merely the penitent soul, but increasingly also heavenly wisdom and the queen of heaven. It is significant that, in this double function, Aseneth serves as a figure with whom readers can identify—female rather than male.[20]

When discussing these developments, the history of religions approach is quick to introduce the concept of mysticism, with the implicit judgment that such modes of thinking are individualistic and do not promote communal solidarity. The structure of the Wisdom of Solomon, however, suggests that it is the product of a school.[21] The allegorical commentary by Philo which is similar in spirit also presupposes a school tradition and hence the continuous existence of a corresponding institution. This tradition is even clearer in Philo's *Quaestiones*.

But Gnosticism required time to become a real mass movement. Philo's Gnostic tendencies, for example, could be confined to the esoteric elite of his school, a kind of secret society. Here the inner circle could withdraw from the public confusion of Jewish life and its institutions to meditate freely. This meditation, however, was primarily communal reflection, in which each individual had a part to play. The Therapeutae (Philo, *Vita contemplativa*) represent a stage in this direction. Philo's *Quaestiones* demonstrate the milieu of the school's training in the art of interpretative meditation.

Philo was a respected member of the Alexandrian Jewish community. Within this society he also represented a different aspect of the wisdom movement: Jewish missionary theology,

20. The rebellious antipatriarchal dimension of the Gnostic program has been discussed by Elaine Pagels, *The Gnostic Gospels* (New York: Random House, 1979). Rose Horman Arthur, *The Wisdom Goddess: Feminine Motifs in Eight Nag Hammadi Documents* (Lanham, Md.: University Press of America, 1984), has shown how a tendency to restore patriarchal values creeps into reformulations of Jewish and pagan Gnostic traditions and texts when they are reformulated by Christian Gnostics, although they retain their democratizing thrust.

21. See the introduction to Georgi, "Weisheit Salomos," 391–95.

usually labelled (quite misleadingly) "apologetics."[22] The ideal of the godlike individual (*theîos anthropos*) was very important for this movement. In diaspora Judaism, even more than in other strata of Hellenistic civilization,[23] this ideal served as a model and stimulus. Despite its aristocratic and elitist overtones, it could be diversified at will and therefore exercised a democratizing influence, not only on political rule but also on the absolute nature of divine authority.

This dispersal and redistribution of power—whether political or divine—is even more evident in the hope that Judaism would become the religion of the whole human race.[24] This aspiration gave wings to Jewish missionary theology, which looked forward not only to God's presence in the midst of a redeemed humanity but also to human participation in the eternal light of God.[25] The statement "They themselves are the judges and righteous kings of the human race"[26] states the office of the messianic king and judge in collective terms. The gifts and privileges that the Jewish Bible ascribed to the eschatological king, Philo ascribed to the eschatological people.[27] Because this nation has learned to exercise self-discipline, it will establish eschatological peace in the human realm and the natural world, as the messianic king of the Bible was expected to do.[28]

In §180 of *De Virtutibus*, another document of missionary theology, Philo describes democracy as the form of government that makes possible the most ordered way of life—that is, the most excellent legal order. In a democracy one encounters education, prudence, discipline, justice, and confidence—in sum, *areté*. Of course Philo, like Aristotle, distinguishes such democracy from ochlocracy in which hold sway

22. See Georgi, *Opponents*, 227–228, 368–89.
23. See Georgi, "Socioeconomic Reasons"; see also the epilogue to Georgi, *Opponents*, 390–422.
24. Georgi, *Opponents*, 148–51.
25. Sybelline Oracles 3.787.
26. Ibid., 782.
27. *De Praemiis et Poenis* 79–84.
28. Ibid., 85–97.

the mob's ignorance, foolishness, extravagance, wickedness, and cowardice—in short, depravity.

Elsewhere[29] Philo states that democracy is the superior form of government because it reflects the order of the universe: equality (*isótēs*), the mother of justice (*dikaiosýnē*), rules in both. In such passages as these,[30] Philo demonstrates his familiarity not only with the political philosophy of Plato and Aristotle but also with the political debate of his own day.[31] Ochlocracy involves what Philo considers purely numerical equality. It gives rise to disorder, lawlessness, and anarchy. True equality is proportionate equality, whereby all members of the community receive their due.

With this preference for equality based on aristocracy (or, better, meritocracy), Philo states his position among his contemporaries (and Paul's) in the debate concerning the ideal form of the state, or, in Wolfson's words, "the principle of government."[32] Readers of the New Testament who think such "political" reflections irrelevant should bear in mind that Philo frequently discusses political issues and political philosophy in the context of ethical or explicitly religious matters. Philo agreed with those in power that the welfare of a community can be promoted only if leadership is in the hands of the best individuals—which means in respect of proportionate equality. The "reactionary" representatives of the *Optimates* insisted that such excellence was demonstrated by natural ties, specifically membership in the senatorial families. The "progressive" representatives of the *Populares,* especially the supporters of Augustus's reforms, claimed superior quality which was demonstrated directly by outstanding service to the state. Both groups—those who leaned toward aristocracy and those

29. *De Specialibus Legibus* iv.237.

30. See Harry A. Wolfson, *Philo: Foundations of Religious Philosophy in Judaism, Christianity, and Islam,* 2 vols. (Cambridge, Mass.: Harvard University Press, 1962), 2:374–95.

31. See the lengthy excursus "Democracy" in F. H. Colson's edition of Philo in the Loeb Classical Library, vol. 8, 437–39.

32. Ibid., 390.

inclined to meritocracy—believed that they were representing true democracy as opposed to false democracy, namely anarchy.

Philo leans more toward meritocracy; in fact, he supports Augustus. He finds biblical support for an elective monarchy.[33] His admiration for Augustus[34] shows that he is a republican in the sense of the Augustan reform of the republic, which had convinced him that Rome was no longer ruled by an aristocratic caste. It was the *princeps* who ruled—the first among equals, the most deserving individual, recognized by all—the *áristos* in the truest sense of the word. In the *Legatio ad Gaium,* therefore, Philo can bring his protest before Gaius Caligula, citing the ideal he found realized in Augustus as a critical principle. Philo's eschatological hopes, discussed above, thus point to a later diversification and collectivization of the virtues and triumphs now still restricted to the few, above all the *princeps.*

It is also true that Philo, outside of the two tractates *Ad Flaccum* and *Legatio ad Gaium,* ventured to criticize Roman politicians and statesmen of his own day (i.e., the post-Augustan period) only indirectly. He concealed this critique in his allegorical commentary, a work intended for the small circle of Jewish Gnostics. He could count on this audience to be receptive to such criticism. The esoteric nature of the material, moreover, guaranteed secrecy. I refer here to the familiar contrast between the figure of Joseph the ideal statesman in the missionary tract *De Josepho*, and Joseph the vain playboy in the allegorical commentary. I agree with Goodenough[35] that this difference is based on political considerations, and above all that Philo wanted to disguise his explicit criticism. I go beyond Goodenough in analyzing more precisely the various groups constituting Philo's audience,

33. See Isaak Heinemann, *Philos griechische und jüdische Bildung* (Darmstadt: Wissenschaftliche Buchgesellschaft, 1962), 184–202.

34. Philo *Legatio ad Gaium* 143–53.

35. Erwin Goodenough, *The Politics of Philo Judaeus* (New Haven: Yale University Press, 1938).

which remained distinct from each other until Philo's later Christian admirers and copyists broke these barriers.[36] I am also convinced that the public description of the ideal statesman in *De Josepho* and the critical picture in the allegorical commentary are related. Philo's ideal statesman reflects the Augustan reform; that is the standard against which Philo measured the politicians of his own day. The actual extent of his negative conclusions he could only intimate in his allegorical commentary. Even such veiled criticism must have been very difficult for him. He and the esoteric group he worked with, in and through his Gnostic writings, exhibited markedly patriarchal tendencies; in comparison to other Gnostic documents they are relatively submissive. Philo often modified the Gnostic traditions he started in this "reactionary" direction.

36. The distinctions in Philo's corpus are discussed in Georgi, *Opponents*, 181–83 n. 59.

2

PAUL AND POLITICAL PRAXIS

THE WISDOM TRADITIONS THAT SHAPED PAUL'S THOUGHT thus merge into political conceptions, especially in discussions of the law, power, authority, righteousness, justice, and effective history. This is no less true when we address the problems of eschatology and God's rulership, frequent topics in Pauline studies. On the contrary, these questions evoke a wealth of political references and allusions. Even in Paul's discussion of grace, one is not far removed from politics, as can be seen at least in his play on the words *cháris* and *eucharistía*.[1] The concrete political applications of Jewish wisdom in the Bible would make a long list. I will restrict myself to a few that are immediately relevant to my theme.

---

1. See Dieter Georgi, *Remembering the Poor* (Decatur: Abingdon Press, forthcoming). I have come to see the political dimensions of these concepts more clearly during the past twenty years.

The Damascus Experience: The Realization of the Conversion of God

The tradition of the Jewish Bible provides many illustrations of change, often quite radical, in ways of thought and action. One encounters a repeated openess to the total transformation of established practice solely on the basis of new experience. Such change is the order of the day in the Jewish Bible; it does not suddenly occur for the first time in the New Testament. It appears above all in the circles of prophets and sages. There is a common tendency, not limited to Christian theology and preaching, to use pseudo-historical arguments in order to demonstrate the uniqueness of Christianity, claiming, as it were, a copyright on revelation. This agenda still imbues biblical scholarship, especially New Testament studies. Jesus and the apostles are made into brilliant innovators. But radicalism to the point of intellectual and political rebellion was not an invention of Jesus or his followers. It is the heritage of the Jewish Bible. Even the Pharisaic party, to which Paul claims to belong (Phil. 3:5), had a program of reform encompassing social and political affairs as well as theology and ethics. The pagan world also made an essential contribution to the critique of religion and religious social criticism.

Paul is well aware of these roots. Even the incident on the road to Damascus, a thoroughly radical experience, he describes in several places by using the critical language of the prophetic and wisdom traditions. Gal. 1:13-16 combines motifs typical of sapiential autobiography[2] and prophetic call,[3] touched up with tints of color from the apocalyptic schema

2. Verses 13-14; cf. Ecclus. 51:13-22; Wisd. Sol. 7:7-22a.
3. For parallels see Jer. 1:5; Isa. 49:1, 5-6; 42:6; 41:9. See also Hans Dieter Betz, *Galatians*, Hermeneia (Philadelphia: Fortress Press, 1979), 69–70. Furthermore, exegesis generally overlooks the motif of being sent to the peoples that is associated with the prophetic call. The prophet represents God before all the peoples and pleads the cause of all the nations before the heavenly council.

of the two aeons.[4] The language of the prophetic call dominates 1 Cor. 15:8-11.[5] Phil. 3:4b-11 stands in the context of a
wisdom testament;[6] in vv. 7-11, however, one finds motifs of
Gnostic revelation.[7] Gnostic language also dominates 2 Cor.
4:6 and its context.[8]

Paul does not understand his Damascus experience as
conversion.[9] He refuses to distort the consequent problems
by engaging in individualistic biographical reflection on his
own past life and defining the questions in terms of personal
guilt. Introspection would be a waste of critical energy. Neither
does he present his experience as a personal shift from one
religious community to another. Paul's experience on the road
to Damascus does indeed unite him with the followers of
Jesus, and this new solidarity gets him into trouble with the
Jewish community. But he does not try to solve the problem
by surrendering his own solidarity or that of the other followers
of Jesus with the covenant history and covenant community
of biblical Judaism. In describing his experience, Paul avoids
speaking of *metánoia/metanoeīn* ("repent[ance]"), a concept
familiar to him from Jewish missionary theology and the
preaching of the diaspora synagogue. Even two decades after
the experience, Paul's own descriptions of his past in Gal.
1:13-14 and Phil. 4:4-6 sound remarkably "impenitent." Instead
of a personal confession of guilt, one finds a concentration

4. For a painstaking analysis of the meaning of *apokalýptein* in the context of
Galatians, see Dieter Lührmann, *Das Offenbarungsverständnis bei Paulus und in
paulinichen Gemeinden*, Wissenschaftliche Monographien zum Alten und Neuen
Testament 16 (Neukirchen: Neukirchener Verlag, 1965), 73–81.

5. The emphasis on the subject's own worthlessness appears also in the calls
of Moses (Exodus 3, 6) and Isaiah (Isaiah 6).

6. The entire fragment comprising 3:2—4:3 and 4:8-9 follows the testament
schema exemplified in the Testaments of the Twelve Patriarchs.

7. See Rudolf Bultmann, "γινῶσκω," in *Theological Dictionary of the New Testament* (*TDNT*), 1:710.

8. The dualistic concept of God in v. 4; the antithesis between "conceal / blind
/ deceive" and "reveal = cause to shine forth" in vv. 2-4; the motifs associated with
light (including *dóxa* ["glory"]) in vv. 4, 6; the *eikōn* ("likeness") concept in v. 4.

9. See Betz, *Galatians*, esp. 64–66.

of critical reflection on the collective foundations of the covenant community and its solidarity—the community to which
Paul and the other followers of Jesus felt they still belonged.

But this very community with all its solidarity had considerable experience with events that forced a particular individual or the whole community to realize that the world had
been turned upside down. Accompanying such a reversal were
substantial theoretical and ethical consequences which needed to be thought through.[10] Paul's experience on the road to
Damascus (which he understood as an encounter with Jesus)
and his consequent solidarity with the followers of Jesus
(whom he had been persecuting) meant that God, by raising
Jesus, again had embraced identification with one who was
accursed.

Galatians 3:13 speaks of Jesus' becoming accursed. It is
not concerned with the subjective guilt or innocence of the
Nazarene. The law Paul cites in this verse curses everyone
who hangs on a tree—including Jesus—quite objectively. According to God's own order the crucifixion of Jesus threatens
humanity in a physical manner which affects all social relations: not only the cultic purity of the land but also its fertility.
The very survival—both religious and socio-economic—of the
covenant community is therefore also threatened. Personal
innocence does nothing to mitigate this curse, as Paul states
even more radically in 2 Cor. 5:21: God makes Jesus, who is
subjectively innocent, not only a sinful individual but identifies
him with sin itself—here even more clearly in a global context
that defines all humanity.

The consequences of Jesus' identification with sin go far
beyond the subjective realm. Paul and the other followers of
Jesus see more than a mere modification of their subjective
interpretation of a given situation they had previously misunderstood. It is more than a shift in their understanding of
themselves and of God. The very essence of the matter is

10. Deuteronomy, Deutero-Isaiah, Ecclesiastes, Job, Daniel, and the Wisdom of
Solomon provide outstanding examples.

changed: it is God who has been transformed. On the other hand, the tradition of biblical Judaism had always experienced such revolutionary experiences of God, not simply as interpretative allusions to prior history, but as divine revelations of primitive and authentic reality.[11] The same holds true for Paul, as his use of scripture demonstrates; one sees this most clearly in the relationship between creation and new creation—when one compares Rom. 1:18—3:20 with Rom. 5–8.

When the Holy One was identified with one who is accursed, the tradition of biblical Judaism encouraged, indeed compelled Paul to call into question both God and God's order. The obvious self-corruption of God and God's order also cast doubt on God's authority, power, and even sovereignty. It was in fact God who demanded this critical review. Throughout the history of biblical Judaism, revolutionary revelation never hesitated before the gates of heaven.[12] At the same time, this revolutionary critique impugned the mundane counterparts of these heavenly phenomena and especially the earthly power structures they supported.

Precisely because they remained in solidarity with the biblical and Jewish community, Jesus' followers and Paul could draw critical energy from that tradition, and could concentrate and strengthen it in a collectivizing direction. Their christological conceptions had communal intentions. The concealed objective of the Jesus movement was to shape collective alternatives to the ongoing community of the people of God. But these alternatives did not aim at a social structure apart from the biblical-Jewish community, and certainly not a new religion. Their aim was a true contrary, a contrary that criticized from within, not without. Paul and other followers of Jesus did not walk out of the Jewish community but conducted a migration within it. They did not embody a new religion but once more a radical rethinking of Judaism to its

11. One sees this most clearly in Deutero-Isaiah and in apocalyptic and Gnostic wisdom, where the identification of the primeval with the endtime figures prominently.

12. This is particularly true with respect to certain branches of the wisdom movement after the appearance of theological wisdom.

very foundations.[13] Because the critical energies behind the Christology and theology of Paul and the early church were collectively oriented, they always had social and political implications. Whether or not Jesus himself was a political activist, the Easter appearances in each case produced a collective consciousness.[14] The alteration on the basis of an experience of God included also the minor deities and their institutions in their critical purview.

The directness with which the early church approached the problem of authority is illustrated by the titles it gave to Jesus, the accursed one now raised and present with his followers. These are the titles that reflect the authority of those who represent God before the covenant people and all humankind: such titles as "prophet," "Christ," "servant," "Son of God," later "son of Man," etc.[15] Some passages even speak of Jesus' rapture or exaltation.[16] The tradition of biblical Judaism also speaks of the rapture or exaltation of mortals (Enoch, Moses, Elijah, Isaiah; later those who are just or wise).[17] But the crucified one is not only unclean (like any corpse) but accursed. To introduce such a person into the heavenly realm desecrates heaven itself. The cross of Jesus has transformed heaven as well as earth. Indeed, heaven is no longer heaven. Paul spells out this transformation in his letters.[18]

13. In the epilogue to Dieter Georgi, *The Opponents of Paul in Second Corinthians* (Philadelphia: Fortress Press, 1986), 346–49, esp. nn. 21–27), I have shown that we cannot speak of "Christians" or "Christianity" in the first century. Initial steps toward religious differentiation are found in Mark, but they do not reach full speed until the last decade of the first century.

14. This is one of the irrefutable insights of David Friedrich Strauss's *Life of Jesus* (1835).

15. See, e.g., Werner Kramer, *Christ, Lord, Son of God,* Studies in Biblical Theology 50 (Naperville, Ill.: Alec R. Allenson, 1966); Klaus Wengst, *Christologische Formeln und Lieder des Urchristentums*, Studien zum Neuen Testament 7 (Gütersloh: Mohn, 1972).

16. The traditional formulas are found in passages such as Phil. 2:9; Acts 2:22; 5:31; 1 Pet. 3:22. The christologies of Hebrews and the Gospel of John are strongly influenced by this tradition.

17. See George Nickelsburg, *Resurrection, Immortality, and Eternal Life in Intertestamental Judaism*, Harvard Theological Studies 26 (Cambridge, Mass.: Harvard University Press, 1972), passim.

18. This theme is developed extensively by the Letter to the Hebrews, a product

But Jesus' followers went even further, elevating the crucified Jesus to the ultimate position of honor: that of God.
This Christology appears in a hymn of the early Hellenistic
Jewish community, which Paul cites almost without change
in Phil. 2:6-11. Here, in language that sounds blasphemous,
the crucified Jesus is both exalted and given the title "Lord."
This is the Septuagint translation of the biblical name of God,
"the name above every name."[19] Paul returned later to this
christological tradition and developed it further in Romans 5,
which I shall discuss below.[20]

In 1 Cor. 16:22, Paul uses the formulaic supplication
"Maranatha." Whatever it meant originally in the context of
the early church's tradition of the Lord's Supper, Paul, in 1
Cor. 11:26 uses this supplication in his own interpretation.
On the one hand, he associates the prayer with Christ's role
as ruler and judge; on the other, he connects it rather crassly
with Jesus' death as point of orientation. Thus he reiterates
once more the blasphemous-sounding tradition cited in Phil.
2:6-11.

When Paul and his associates understand their christological experience as demanding a reversal of the concept of

---

of the Pauline school. Hebrews 13:12-16 uses the metaphor of leaving the sacred
precincts of the wilderness camp to enter the unholy desert beyond to represent
Jesus' exaltation to the heavenly realm as high priest, thus identifying heaven with
chaos. This identification is suggested in chap. 4 and explicit in 10:19-21. The next
verses (10:22-25) anticipate 13:13-17.

19. See Dieter Georgi, "Der vorpaulinische Hymnus Phil. 2, 6-11," in *Zeit und
Geschichte: Dankesgabe an Rudolf Bultmann zum 80. Geburtstag,* ed. Erich Dinkler
(Tübingen: J. C. B. Mohr [Paul Siebeck], 1964), 263–93.

20. Blasphemy is a central feature of the biblical tradition from the very beginning.
The theological conflicts, often quite radical, that historical-critical study has identified behind the biblical text included charges of blasphemy—variously situated and
directed, of course, depending on the prevailing perspective. The representatives of
Yahwism in the northern kingdom considered themselves orthodox, while the story
of the golden calf (Exodus 32) in its present satirical and polemical form imputes
terrible blasphemy to them. They in turn undoubtedly accused the Jerusalem cult
of blasphemous innovations. On the complex history of this tradition, see Frank M.
Cross, *Canaanite Myth and Hebrew Epic* (Cambridge, Mass.: Harvard University Press,
1973), 73–75. The book of Job, to cite another example, is also not lacking in
blasphemies.

God, they do so compelled by their interpretation of the biblical-Jewish experiential heritage, a critical tradition indeed.
Therefore, this conception is not to be seen as a theory Paul
is advancing but as the reflected praxis of both Paul and his
forebears. Praxis is also suggested by the liturgical character
of the early hymns to Christ and the tradition of christological
creeds, as well as the tradition of the Lord's Supper. All of
these features reflect not the experience and conduct of an
individual but the praxis of the community. And this reflection
in turn leads directly back into praxis.

The dominant role of praxis in Paul's thought is further
illustrated by the fact that he never refers to his experience
on the road to Damascus as an isolated biographical incident.
When he alludes to it, it always bears directly on the specific
issue under discussion. And this issue always concerns the
community addressed. The Damascus episode is meaningful
for Paul only because it has collective implications and mo-
mentum. This is true even in Phil. 3:7-11, where the first person
pronoun could be misunderstood as signaling an autobiography. But both the style of the passage (which reflects the
"testament" form of wisdom literature) and the Gnostic ideas
it incorporates show that Paul is making a general statement.
These elements in combination provide a model with significant societal implications, an alternative to the various other
models hinted at—not only Pharisaism but also the Judaizing
model of the opponents addressed in this fragment. The passage even deals with Jewish missionary theology, the context
whence Paul borrows the testament form.

This carefully considered critical praxis appears not only
in Paul's missionary work on behalf of Jesus—a result of his
Damascus experience—but also in his tendency to give this
work collegial shape. This collegiality went back at least to
Paul's stay at Antioch (Barnabas!). It even appears to increase
in the final phase of Paul's missionary activity, misleadingly
called "independent." A strong bond of unity with each congregation, from the day of its founding, informs Paul's work
and thought. This solidarity appears in all of his letters—most

strikingly in the ambiguous "we" of 1 Thessalonians and the fragments of 2 Corinthians.

The socio-political nature of the traditions borrowed by the early church and by Paul, together with their emphasis on praxis, suggest that it is wrong to accuse the first-century followers of Jesus of retreating from the "secular" world and its political life into "eschatology." Each of the contexts in which Paul refers to his Damascus experience involves criticism of religious concepts that have socio-political relevance and impact. In Galatians, one finds this association primarily in the latter part of chap. 3 and in chap. 4, which discuss the law as *paidagōgós* ("guardian"), the *stoicheía toū kósmou* ("elemental spirits of the universe"), and freedom. Philippians 3 addresses similar questions. Practical discussion of social and economic issues characterizes 1 Corinthians in its entirety. I shall return to a more detailed discussion of the politically significant concept of *sōma* ("body") which Paul develops in this letter, especially in chaps. 12 and 15. From the fragments of 2 Corinthians (in anticipation of what will follow), one may single out the debate over tradition, performance, and achievement—phenomena of great importance for Hellenistic society as a whole. Paul's personal experiences and his subsequent reflections on divine authority and order all have concrete impact. They suggest alternative designs together with their social implications. These designs and implications are in contrast to an established world order marked by wide consensus, transcending religious divisions, about the nature and relationship of high and low.

First Thessalonians: God Joins the People

In 1 Thessalonians, Paul demonstrates that both he and his readers are dealing with a transformed God. In 1 Thess. 4:13-18, Paul describes the awaited parousia of Jesus, the "Lord."

[13]But we would not have you ignorant, brethren, concerning those who are asleep, that you may not grieve as others do who have no hope. [14]For since we believe that Jesus died and rose again, even so, through Jesus, God will bring with him those who have fallen asleep. [15]For this we declare to you by the word of the Lord, that we who are alive, who are left until the coming of the Lord, shall not precede those who have fallen asleep. [16]For the Lord himself will descend from heaven with a cry of command, with the archangel's call, and with the sound of the trumpet of God. And the dead in Christ will rise first, [17]then we who are alive, who are left, shall be caught up together with them in the clouds to meet the Lord in the air; and so we shall always be with the Lord. [18]Therefore comfort one another with these words.

The cry of command and angel's call, the people's approach, and the clouds recall the Sinai theophany as elaborated in Jewish tradition.[21] The meeting with the Lord described in v. 17 takes place after the faithful who are still alive are caught up into the heavens. The model for this phenomenon is the "legitimizing" ceremony "in which persons of high rank were formally brought by the citizens into the city."[22] Dibelius[23] points out that the imagery Paul uses here implies that the faithful ascend into the heavens in order to bring the Lord down to earth. They meet him outside their city to lead

21. Jacques Dupont, *ΣYN XPIΣTΩ: L'union avec le Christ suivant Saint Paul* (Bruges: L'Abbaye de Saint André, 1952), 45, 68–69, 97–98; but see also Ernest Best, *A Commentary on the First and Second Epistles to the Thessalonians* (London: A. & C. Black, 1972), pp. 196–202, esp. 199.

22. Erik Peterson, *apántēsis* ("meeting"), in *TDNT*, 1:380.

23. Martin Dibelius, *An die Thessalonicher I, II, An die Philipper*, Handbuch zum Neuen Testament 11 (Tübingen: J. C. B. Mohr [Paul Siebeck], 1937), 28. Dibelius discusses an earlier study by Peterson that is fundamental to the article cited above and to several other discussions of the same text.

him down and escort him through the gates of their "city"—this earth—to celebrate his arrival.[24]

The significance of this Lord's legitimacy and authority is made explicit by the parallelism between 1 Thess. 4:15-17 and 1 Thess. 2:1-13. The welcoming of the Lord is reflected in the Thessalonians' reception of the Lord's ambassador, Paul. The peculiarity of the dignity of the apostle in chap. 2 parallels the peculiarity of the expectation of a Jesus from heaven whose welcome resembles and surpasses that given the rulers of the world. But Jesus surpasses them because he resembles his comical messengers, of whom Paul is one among many. For the Paul of 1 Thessalonians, eschatological reality means that the fools take the field and make fools of the would-be mighty. One must bear in mind that 2:1-13 anticipates 4:15-17. The revolution has already begun to transform not only the social situation but also its power structures and this transformation has gained legitimacy. The final saturnalia have already begun.

In 1 Thess. 5:8, Paul plays with the prophetic words of Isa. 59:17. This text from Trito-Isaiah is one of the many biblical passages that draw on the ancient Near Eastern myth of a primordial battle between the gods.[25] Here, the myth is interpreted eschatologically. The biblical symbol of God as an armed champion in the holy war that establishes, preserves, or restores creation is transferred in toto by 1 Thess. 5:8 to the community as a whole—it is literally democratized. This shift incorporates and develops the proclivity for resistance inherent in apocalypticism and Gnosticism. The company of Jesus in its collective life, characterized by the triad of faith,

24. It should be added that while the very sketchy parallel in 1 Cor. 15:51-52 sheds little light on the imagery, it does not contradict 1 Thess. 4:17. In any case, Rom. 11:25-31, another related passage, seems clearly to refer to this present world; it does not mention the resurrection or a heavenly realm. Revelation 21–22, a textual complex dating from a later period of the early church, likewise describes the descent to earth of the heavenly Jerusalem. It is commonly asserted that Jewish eschatology always relates to the present world whereas "Christian" eschatology looks for a transcendent world to come; this claim is hard to square with the textual evidence.

25. See the discussion above, 7–11.

love, and hope, is engaged in battle. This battle creates the world—or better, in the eschatological context, creates it anew. The critical event for the fate of the universe does not come to pass in heaven with God or among the gods. It does not involve the mighty of this world. It has nothing to do with force or violence. It takes place within and through a community held together by faith, love, and hope.[26]

Despite the eschatological ambience of the discussion in 4:13-18 and 5:1-11, this democratizing emphasis on a historically identifiable community prevents us from assigning Paul's words to some kind of religious ghetto, whether of absolute transcendence or of pure subjectivity. Neither are we dealing with sociological isolation within the ghetto of a sect, despite the emphasis on "we." The appeal to "peace and security" cited in 1 Thess. 5:3 is an ironic allusion to the official theology and propaganda of the *Pax Romana*. "Peace and security" is the motto of the Roman world after the establishment of the Principate, that is, after Augustus' "miraculous" termination of the civil war and his establishment of "universal peace."[27]

One must also not overlook the political and social background of the Isaiah passage that Paul draws upon in 5:8. Hanson describes it as follows: "The picture of the social order sketched by the indictment and lament in verses 1-15a

26. In his summary introduction to the letter (1:3), Paul already uses the triad of *pístis, agápē,* and *elpís* to describe the life of the Christian community as a gift and a mission. He adopted this triad from a tradition that may even antedate the Christian church. Its traditional nature is especially clear in 5:8, where Paul is forced to join a doublet with a triplet. For further discussion, see Dibelius, *An die Thessalonicher,* 29–30, and Hans Conzelmann, *1 Corinthians,* Hermeneia (Philadelphia: Fortress Press, 1975), 229–31, with bibliographical material in the religio-historical discussion.

27. See Klaus Wengst, *Pax Romana and the Peace of Jesus Christ* (Philadelphia: Fortress Press, 1987), esp. 19–21, 77–78. It is interesting in the present context that Augustus and his theologians, especially Vergil, could use the form of the theomachy, in which the forces of chaos are defeated and heavenly order is restored (now interpreted eschatologically), to describe the events leading to the "restoration of the Republic." Wengst's discussion notwithstanding, this official theology and propaganda exercised its fascination beyond the limits of the upper classes. The Caesarcult had a religious attraction for broader circles as well.

is that of the complete breakdown of justice and righteous-ness."²⁸ Hanson shows that one of the reasons Trito-Isaiah introduces the myth of the divine warrior is to lend a global dimension not only to the immediate discussion but also to his program for the future. The same is true for Paul's use of the Trito-Isaiah passage. The entire letter is anything but private or sectarian and the global, even cosmic, dimension is especially clear in 4:15. One may dispute Hanson's further claim that Trito-Isaiah is already using the myth to establish a dualistic schema.²⁹ Whatever conclusions one reaches about Trito-Isaiah, Paul in any case exhibits a clear demythologizing interest in establishing its concrete historical application—not in 5:10a alone but throughout the entire letter, and particularly in his direct use of Isa. 59:17 in 5:8.

I should also note that, in the context of biblical Judaism, *sōtēría* ("salvation") and its equivalents clearly refer to concrete historical events, usually affecting groups rather than individuals. This is true even of eschatological texts. Moreover the same situation applies in the Hellenistic gentile realm. The concrete historical meaning of *sōtēría/sōtēr* ("salvation/savior"), and especially the collective aspect, became increasingly dominant after the battle of Actium. During the first century, this concept exerted enormous power in the Roman sphere of influence (including Thessalonica and Corinth, where 1 Thessalonians was probably written). One virtually trips over it in the form of inscriptions of gratitude honoring the deeds of "saviors." And, as has been suggested by me elsewhere,³⁰ eschatology, albeit in the form of realized eschatology, reached it zenith in Augustan theology and the Caesar-cult to which it gave birth.

Realized eschatology also appears in 1 Thess. 5:1-8. Here Paul critically modifies his reasoning in 4:13-18 by using the

28. Paul D. Hanson, *The Dawn of Apocalyptic* (Philadelphia: Fortress Press, 1975), 132.
29. Ibid., 126–34.
30. Dieter Georgi, "Who Is the True Prophet?" in *Christians Among Jews and Gentiles,* ed. George W. Nickelsburg, George W. MacRae (Philadelphia: Fortress Press, 1986), 100–126.

terminology of Gnosticism (5:5) and the mysteries (5:6-7) to restate his previous argument in terms of the present. It is noteworthy that the biblical allusion in 5:8 and its christological interpretation in 5:10 both avoid the future tense. The triad of faith, hope, and love together with the biblical text lead Paul to speak of hope of salvation and, in the next verse, of obtaining salvation. According to v. 10, however, the substance of this salvation, life with Jesus, is a reality that has already begun, though it is not yet finished. In this sense 5:8-10 goes beyond 4:14. It is also clear that life with Jesus is not a paradise of milk and honey: it demands responsibility within the community, described at more length in v. 11 and in the parenetic sections preceding and following. One is dealing here with an alternative model of society in outline.

The criticism Paul embarks on in 1 Thessalonians, like the resistance movements of apocalypticism and Gnosticism, addresses more than a religious world and concerns more than a single political figure. As 1 Thess. 2:1-13 makes abundantly clear, Paul criticizes the political structures of the world concurrently with the motives and criteria that inform them. This antithesis, too, is formulated dialogically; it is not imposed from without.[31]

The justification is stated in 5:10. The death of Jesus is an act of solidarity that establishes life and community—not in spite of death, but through death. Less otherworldliness, not more, marks the pith and essence of this more than merely religious critique of first-century politics and society. The divinization of the Caesar is countered by the humanization of the Pauline (biblical) God.

The consequences of this argument are stated in 5:10b and 11, a plea for mutual encouragement and constructive treatment. Here, in the verb *oikodomeîn*, a concept appears

---

31. The individualizing Gnostic assertions concerning *sōtēría* (see Erich Förster, *sózō* ("to save") *TDNT*, 7:1002, 1019–20) likewise have an element of protest and thus a social and political dimension. For the discussion below, it is significant that Cicero conceived of the state as an edifice and the statesman as an architect, whose work is termed *aedificare*.

that will be important later in the discussion of the body of Christ. This passage already hints at the political dimensions of the building/body symbol, thereby laying the groundwork for 1 Corinthians 12 and Romans 12.

3

PAUL'S ALTERNATIVE UTOPIA

Galatians: The Cross as Parody

In Galatians 3 and 4, Paul presupposes the unity of the world as a reflection of the unity of God and the unity of God's universal law. This unity was an article of faith not only for Jewish missionary theology but also throughout much of the Hellenistic world. At the same time Paul presupposes the experience of law as a liberating agent: negatively, in chaps. 3 and 4 (the claim of law as liberation through education), positively in chaps. 5 and 6 (law as liberation through love). In both chapters, he speaks of the world as a single, homogeneous entity: the law does not apply exclusively to Israel but to the world as a whole. This is especially clear in what he says about the *stoicheīa toū kósmou* in 4:3 and 4:9. The unity of God is the theme of 3:20. In 3:23-24 Paul associates the law with pedagogy in an ironic treatment of Hellenistic ideals. He develops this association in 4:1-3, where the law is sarcastically identified with slavery instead of deliverance.

The idea of the world as a single whole is found elsewhere; for example in Philo *De opificio mundi* 171. It is commonplace in Hellenistic philosophy.[1] Alexander the Great and his many *epigoni* should also be cited as representing a very activistic concept of the world's unity as a liberating and unifying idea, especially in connection with universal law and education. Plutarch's biography of Alexander documents the vitality of the Alexander legend in the New Testament period.[2]

Concerning the relationship between education and society, Jaeger has shown that *paideía* is synonymous with culture.[3] By the time of Alexander at the latest, it is this *paideía* rather than biological ancestry that distinguishes those who are civilized from the barbarians. Barbarism now means lack of education and culture.[4] Furthermore, it is especially important to note that in the Hellenistic period the king, and then the royal or divine individual, comes to be the embodiment of the law.[5] "Following [Aristotle], people came to think of education as an attribute making mortals like the gods; for the fruit of *paideía* is the ability to make judicious plans."[6]

It does not appear that Paul's opponents in Galatia, whatever their teaching and praxis may have been, called into question these social presuppositions in any fundamental

1. Compare Plato *Timaeus* 32C—33A; Aristotle *De caelo* i.8. For examples from the Stoics, see Johannes von Arnim, ed., *Stoicorum Veterum Fragmenta* (Leipzig: Teubner, 1903–24), II:530–33. Also important—especially for the matter under discussion—is the eclectic Pseudo-Aristotelian *De mundo*.

2. Philo's apologetic writings, in particular *De opificio mundi*, may be cited as impressive examples of works associating law with the unity of the world. The Stoics' cosmologically oriented concept of law continues themes found in the great systematic philosophers Democritus, Plato, and Aristotle. The Stoics also treat law and freedom as belonging together. Kleinknecht summarizes this understanding briefly but well in *Theological Dictionary of the New Testament* (*TDNT*), 4:1032-34, "*nómos.*" Law is a reflection of divinity—for many, it is in fact God's-self (ibid., 1034).

3. Werner Jaeger, *Paideia*, 4th ed. (Oxford: Basil Blackwell Mott, 1954-1956), passim.

4. W. Spoerri, in *Der kleine Pauly* (Stuttgart: Druckenmüller, 1964), 1:1546–47.

5. Kleinknecht, "*nómos,*" 1025–26.

6. Georg Bertram, "*paideúō,*" in *TDNT*, 5:602-3; see also Erwin Goodenough, "The Political Philosophy of Hellenistic Kingship," *Yale Classical Studies* 1 (1928): 53–102.

sense. At least this is so in Paul's estimation as one sees above all in Paul's discussion of the *stoicheîa toû kósmou* in chap. 4.[7]

The dense argumentation in the stylized and pointed account of the Antioch conflict in Gal. 2:14-21 establishes the thesis that will be elaborated upon in chaps. 3 and 4.

[14]But when I [Paul] saw that they were not straightforward about the truth of the gospel, I said to Cephas before them all, "If you, though a Jew, live like a Gentile and not like a Jew, how can you compel the Gentiles to live like Jews?" [15]We ourselves, who are Jews by birth and not Gentile sinners, [16]yet who know that a man is not justified by works of the law but through faith in Jesus Christ, even we have believed in Christ Jesus, in order to be justified by faith in Christ, and not by works of the law, because by works of the law shall no one be justified. [17]But if, in our endeavor to be justified in Christ, we ourselves were found to be sinners, is Christ then an agent of sin? Certainly not! [18]But if I build up again those things which I tore down, then I prove myself a transgressor. [19]For I through the law died to the law, that I might live to God. [20]I have been crucified with Christ; it is no longer I who live, but Christ who lives in me; and the life I now live in the flesh I live by faith in the Son of God, who loved me and gave himself for me. [21]I do not nullify the grace of God; for if justification were through the law, then Christ died to no purpose.

7. The fact that the debate over the nature of these opponents is still unresolved is not surprising in light of the dense and complex argumentation of the letter and the absence of any clear quotations from their teaching. Brinsmead has published a very careful analysis of the problem (Bernhard Brinsmead, *Galatians—Dialogical Response to Opponents*, Society of Biblical Literature Dissertation Series, 65 [Chico: Scholars Press, 1983]). Even if the opponents were more Gnostic than Brinsmead allows, they were concerned with surmounting the world.

The very examples of Peter and Paul make it clear that neither *phýsis* nor *nómos* (*érga toū nómou*)[8] has the power to establish a social bond (*dikaioūsthai*).[9] What both apostles experienced—in different places, but ultimately bringing them together—has shown that this power is given instead by the *pístis Iēsoū Christoū* (Gal. 2:16). Because they have had this experience (*eidótes*), an Easter experience for both, they have come to believe that Jesus is the royal Messiah.[10]

Certainly Gal. 2–4 has in mind primarily the Jewish Torah. But Paul's critical catch phrase (*dikaioūsthai/dikaiosýnē*) *ex érgōn nómou* (Gal. 2:16; cp. 3:2, 5, 10) is not attested anywhere as a Jewish byword let alone a party slogan. One is confronted

8. See the discussion in n. 11 below.

9. The text on which the argument in v. 16 is based is Psalm 142 LXX (Eng. 143). This psalm speaks at the outset of the questioning or denial of social solidarity on the part of the psalmist's accusers, followed by the restoration of this solidarity solely through the *dikaiosýnē* / *éleos* / *kataphygē* / *hodós* / *ónoma* of the covenant God. This restoration is what is meant by the *dikaioūsthai enōpión sou* (the latter phrase being dropped by Paul himself in 2:17 for the sake of clarity) that no human being can achieve independently.

10. There is no reason to associate *pístis Iēsoū Christoū* and *episteúsamen* with the same subjects—specifically Peter and Paul—as though both referred to *their* faith in Jesus as Messiah. That would be an unnecessary tautology. Exegetes attempt to avoid such a purely tautological interpretation by taking *eidótes* to suggest that the noun *pístis* in v. 16 is meant in a theoretical and dogmatic sense and the verb *episteúsamen* in the same verse refers to a practical and existential application of this knowledge about faith. In this combination, then, Gal. 2:16 has become a key passage for the understanding of *pístis* as "faith in" and especially for the interpretation of the genitive as an objective genitive.

The absolute usage of *pístis*, however, predominates in Galatians. Furthermore, the concept is hypostatized in 3:23-25, where it can be understood as being synonymous with Jesus. One may therefore ask, with respect to the two exceptional passages where *pístis* appears with a genitive, whether the genitive should not be interpreted as subjective or even explicative—in other words, whether the phrase does not mean "the faith of Jesus" or even "the faith that is Jesus." If so, in 2:16 and 3:22 the term *pístis* would denote the trust (or even better "loyalty") of Jesus, indeed the trust and loyalty Jesus stands for; and this establishes and preserves social solidarity. This interpretation would agree with what is said about Jesus in chaps. 3 and 4.

For criticism of the current understanding of *pístis*, see also Richard B. Hays, *The Faith of Jesus Christ: An Investigation of the Narrative Substructure of Galatians 3:1—4:11*, Society of Biblical Literature Dissertation Series 56 (Chico: Scholars Press, 1983).

then with a polemical expression coined by Paul himself. The attempt to associate it specifically with the Pharisaic or even rabbinic view of the law must be considered a failure.[11] Paul must have something more universal in mind. Now he has already expanded his horizon in 2:18. Here the "I" no longer refers to Paul as an individual; at the very least, it stands for all who believe in Jesus, Jews *and* Gentiles, possibly even (as in Rom. 7:7-25) the whole human race. Paul goes beyond the purely Jewish experience of the Torah to include Gentile experience, an experience that has not been exposed directly to the Jewish law. This tendency to enlarge the scope of the argument becomes stronger in chap. 3 and is absolutely unmistakeable in chap. 4. Thus the phrase *érga nómou* describes a dimension of experience open to all.

If one follows Dewey[12] in assuming that *érga nómou* refers to an existential world that is causative in nature (*ek!*), it is reasonable to interpret the genitive in this phrase as a *gen. auctoris* and regard the *érga nómou* as actions not only enjoined but also brought about by the law. This understanding likewise agrees with the description in chap. 3 of the magical power of the law, sensitively analyzed by Dewey, to which I shall return shortly. Looking ahead, one observes that 3:10 refers to a scripture text which addresses the establishment of a society under law at the time of the occupation of Canaan

11. This has been shown above all by Ed Parish Sanders in his book *Paul and Palestinian Judaism* (Philadelphia: Fortress Press, 1977). In his article "Gesetzeswerke" (published in his *Probleme paulinischer Theologie* [Stuttgart: Kohlhammer, 1955], 31–74), Ernst Lohmeyer has proposed rendering this phase by means of "Dienst des Gesetzes" ("service of the law"); but this suggestion, too, is questionable. What Paul has in mind is something very concrete, which is more than one can say of the expression "service of the law," even though it takes one further than the translation "works of the law."

Lohmeyer's argument has been developed further by Joseph B. Tyson, " 'Works of Law' in Galatians," *Journal of Biblical Literature* 92 (1973): 425–31. In "Spirit and Letter in Paul" (Ph.D. diss., Harvard University, 1982), 20–40, 43–73, Arthur Dewey has shown the way to a better understanding of the text by suggesting that in Galatians 2 and 3 one should speak of two different ways of life, one characterized by *érga nómou*, the other by *akoè písteōs*.

12. See n. 11.

by the Israelites. It is reasonable therefore to understand *érga nómou* as the social and cultural achievements (not just religious acts), not only ordained but also brought about by law—in principle, by any law.[13] Such an understanding would also agree with the understanding of *érga* in the Greek and Hellenistic world.[14]

For the first time in the extant corpus of Pauline literature, Gal. 2:18 points out that the law (here, return to the law) makes one a transgressor.[15] The law itself thus effects what it purposes to prevent. In the very next verse (2:19), the law is associated with death and set in antithesis to life.

This antithesis continues in Gal. 3:1-14:

> O foolish Galatians! Who has bewitched you, before whose eyes Jesus Christ was publicly portrayed as crucified? [2]Let me ask you only this: Did you receive the Spirit by works of the law, or by hearing with faith? [3]Are you so foolish? Having begun with the Spirit, are you now ending with the flesh? [4]Did you experience so many things in vain?—if it really is in vain. [5]Does he who supplies the Spirit to you and works miracles among you do so by works of the law, or by hearing with faith?

13. Apart from circumcision (esp. in 6:12), Paul does not mention any requirement that is specifically biblical or is enjoined by Jewish law. The catalog in 4:10 is utterly universal. Here we have a list of calendrical taboos, which Paul naturally derides as superstition. The verb *paratēréō* ("observe") does not limit the reference to cultic rituals, a restriction in meaning erroneously proposed by Hans Dieter Betz, *Galatians*, Hermeneia (Philadelphia: Fortress Press, 1979), 218. (Cf. Harald Riesenfeld, *paratēréō*, in *TDNT*, 8:147.) In any case, the ancient world, including the first century, knew nothing of the strict distinction between religion and the secular world.

14. See Georg Bertram and H. Kleinknecht, "*érgon*," in *TDNT*, 2:635–36, esp. n. 5. The Roman understanding of *opus*/*opera* is very similar.

15. In *parabátēs*, Paul chooses a term that only rarely has the meaning "transgressor." The verb *parabaínō* and the noun *parábasis*, however, are frequently used for the transgression of laws and ordinances. There can be no question of a restriction to cultic ordinances in this context (see Johannes Schneider, "*parabaínō*," in *TDNT*, 5:736–42). Paul does not select here a term limited to the cult, but one with more general associations.

[6]Thus Abraham "believed God, and it was reckoned to him as righteousness." [7]So you see that it is men of faith who are the sons of Abraham. [8]And the scripture, forseeing that God would justify the Gentiles by faith, preached the gospel beforehand to Abraham, saying, "In you shall all the nations be blessed." [9]So then, those of faith are blessed with Abraham who had faith.

[10]For all who rely on works of the law are under a curse; for it is written, "Cursed be every one who does not abide by all things written in the book of the law, and do them." [11]Now it is evident that no one is justified before God by the law; for "Whoever is righteous will live by faith"; [12]but the law does not rest on faith, for "Whoever does the works of the law will live by them." [13]Christ redeemed us from the curse of the law, having become a curse for us—for it is written, "Cursed be every one who hangs on a tree"—[14]that in Christ Jesus the blessing of Abraham might come upon the Gentiles, that we might receive the promise of the Spirit through faith.

In 3:1, Paul—with what appears to be rhetorical exaggeration—initially associates only his opponents with wizardry. Beginning with v. 2, however, the law itself and the results it accomplishes are drawn increasingly into the context of wizardry and magic. This development culminates in 3:10-13.[16] According to 3:10a, all who ground their existence in *érga nómou* are under the curse.[17] Verse 10b cites Deut. 27:26

16. See Dewey, "Spirit and Letter in Paul."

17. This cannot refer only to the Jews, just as Gal. 3:8 cannot refer only to the Gentiles. Either limitation would contradict the argument of Gal. 2:15-21, which brings Jews and Gentiles together. In 3:8a, *tà éthnē* refers to the nations as a whole, as in the scriptural quotation in 8b (*pace* Betz, *Galatians*, 144). This generalizing interpretation of v. 10a is also supported by the choice of *hósoi*. Otherwise—i.e., if the Gentiles were not included in 3:10-12—what 3:13 and 4:4 say about the subjection of Jesus to the curse and the law, which is the basis and cause of deliverance, would likewise not include the Gentiles; it would only apply to the Jews. As it is, Jesus' subjection affects all people, Jews and Gentiles alike. This is also stated in 3:14.

in support of this conclusion. Moreover, one must not overlook the interpretative extension of this citation in v. 12b. Here Paul contrasts the point of the Deuteronomy passage to Hab. 2:4, at the same time using the verb *zḗsetai,* which in 12b means something like "derives his existence." Precisely because it is scripture, the law is bewitching.[18] It constrains people not only to stay within the law but to act, and it is this constraint to act, to achieve, that is the curse of the law. There is no escape. No one can remain an inactive bystander: one is condemned to act, condemned to achieve results.

In Hellenistic Judaism, the written form of the law and of tradition are signs of their salvific importance for the world. For Paul, however, in Galatians 3,[19] and not only in 2 Corinthians 3, this scriptural form is a sign of the law's magical power and its spell, of captivity and the curse—a theme that will be stated more pointedly in 3:22.

Scripture is divided into a power to bless and a power to curse. This division is noted also by 3:19, but from a somewhat different perspective.[20] Dewey has developed this theme of the "double magic of Scripture" in a fine manner.[21] "The law is not dead, but lethal for those who are (*eisín*) *ex érgōn nómou.*"[22] Here Paul shows that he has learned from Jewish

Restricting this verse to the Gentiles would mean that Paul considered faith to be the characteristic distinguishing the Gentiles from the Jews, a conclusion that would fly in the face of the entire Pauline argument, especially the conclusion of chap. 2. The notion that the Jews were the rear guard in faith is contradicted by the faithful followers of Jesus in Jerusalem and Palestine, not to mention Paul himself. Of course they are not in the vanguard, either.

18. Dewey, "Spirit and Letter in Paul," 61–63.

19. Dewey (ibid., 59–60) has shown, with particular reference to Paul's treatment of the citation from Deut. 27:26, that this passage is intended to emphasize the written form of the law and the association of this form with the curse.

20. Insofar as the *graphḗ* is direct prophetic discourse, basically equivalent to immediate oral communication that opens the future, it is seen in a positive light, as a promising word. Insofar as it is mediated by a written form, through angels or Moses, it is a curse. It establishes and seals a social bond oriented to performance and achievement. In this a common fate is set, a curse that bars the future.

21. Dewey, "Spirit and Letter in Paul," 52–69.

22. Ibid., 62. Dewey also points out the connection of this notion with the practice of cursing common in antiquity (59, 62).

Gnosticism, which speaks of the existence of a powerful antiworld. This antiworld pretends to be a real creation but is not; it promises life and success but brings chaos, impotence, and catastrophe.[23] The Nag Hammadi documents provide evidence that in the New Testament period, Gnostic Jewish texts were beginning to subject the biblical Creator-God to this dualistic critique. The Apocalypse of Adam (V), for example, calls the Creator-God of Genesis *pantokrátōr* (69:7), Saklas (74:3-4, 7), and the God of the Powers (77:4). He has the "authority of death" (67:12-13). Noah calls on his sons to serve this God "in fear and slavery" (72:21-22). Noah's descendants did the will of this demiurge (74:18-19). Pantokrator / Saklas differs from the eternal God (64:13-14, etc.), who is the God of truth (65:13) and the living God (84:9-10).[24]

23. The Wisdom of Solomon speaks of this antiworld as being based on a *synthḗkē* ("covenant") with death (1:16); it has its own *nómos tēs dikaiosýnēs* (2:11). It is typically *ischýs* ("force / strength") that represents this "law of righteousness" of the visible, tangible world, the "violence" that demonstratively rages against the righteous. The last section of the book identifies this antiworld with Egypt. This identification is not surprising from the perspective of the biblical exodus narrative, but it is remarkable against the historical background of the book. Even more than Pharaonic Egypt, Ptolemaic Egypt, when compared to similar entities, had become a land that had developed a model society with an astonishingly liberal legal system. This system was highly esteemed, not least by the enormous Jewish community in Egypt—as its very numbers, comprising both immigrants and proselytes, attest. The Letter of Aristeas, a Jewish missionary tract, is an impressive document of Jewish esteem for Ptolemaic Egypt as a power representing civilization and order. In the age of Augustus Egypt even became a model of Roman administration. Nevertheless, in the New Testament period the Egyptian Jew Philo treats Egypt as a symbol of chaos, especially in his allegorical commentaries. Here, too, one sees the Gnostic tendency to unmask the established order as chaos.

24. The most recent treatment of this work will be found in Rose H. Arthur, *The Wisdom Goddess: Feminine Motifs in Eight Nag Hammadi Documents* (Lanham, Md.: University Press of America, 1984), 21–36. Arthur includes a comparison with the Tractate on the Exegesis of the Soul. Such comparison makes the non-Christian character of the Apocalypse of Adam quite clear. I agree with the conclusion of George W. MacRae, who considers this Gnostic apocalypse to be a document without any Christian influence, contemporary with the New Testament. What MacRae says is important for the following discussion: "The Redeemer Myth of the Apocalypse of Adam grew out of late Jewish speculations that were fostered by the syncretistic atmosphere of the Near East around the time when Christianity made its appearance."

In Galatians, Paul does not go along with this dualistic division of the deity; he does, nevertheless, incorporate the dualism into his concept of scripture.[25] This conflict among competing legal obligations reflects a dichotomy in the experience of faith with respect to the world, a division at odds with the social unity talked up by contemporary Hellenistic ideology. It is not simply that society fails to deliver what it promises. The world, and above all the world as an ordered society, enslaves and destroys. Gnostic wisdom had paved the way for the critique of the law to which Paul finds himself driven, but there are no true contemporary parallels.[26]

The Wisdom of Solomon,[27] Philo,[28] and above all the Apocalypse of Adam[29] speak of individuals who invade the demonic realm of the evil world in which the human race is entrapped, bringing revelation and salvation. In Gal. 3:13, discussed above, Paul similarly depicts Jesus as entering the satanic realm of the curse of the law.[30] Paul describes here

---

(From "The Coptic Gnostic Apocalypse of Adam," *Heythrop Journal* 6 [1965]: 27-35; see also his "The Apocalypse of Adam Reconsidered," in *The Society of Biblical Literature: One Hundred Eighth Annual Meeting, Seminar Papers* [1972], 2:573–80.)

25. The Apocalypse of Adam provides a parallel, in that 84:10-11 describes the persecutors of the Gnostics as "lawless," thereby implying that on the side of the eternal God there is something like a law opposing the demonic will of Saklas. The latter is not explicitly granted the title "law." Immediately germane to the subject under discussion is the fact that shortly after the passage quoted it is said that the same persecutors come under the spell of the "will of the Powers" and are forced to "serve" them. The similarity to Gal. 4:1-10 is very clear.

26. By sarcastically describing the law as a *paídagogós* ("pedagogue") in Gal. 3:24-25 and 4:13 and thus excoriating the presumptuous claims of Hellenistic education, Paul takes up and intensifies the criticism of education found in the popular philosophy of the Stoics and Cynics (see Betz, *Galatians*, 177–78) by adding a mythological dimension. I have discussed this critique of education found in early Gnosticism in my "Das Wesen der Weisheit nach der Weisheit Salomos," in *Gnosis und Politik*, ed. Jacob Taubes (Paderborn: Schöningh, 1984), 78–81.

27. The embodiment of wisdom happens in the wise.

28. The *Logos* is God's revelatory and saving agent.

29. Heavenly emissaries, from the three angels, Eve and Adam (and of course Seth), and the various bringers of light to the revealers/saviors described in a self-contained poem of equal age (77:27—82:19) work as divine agents.

30. Dewey, "Spirit and Letter in Paul," 65–66: "The lack of a connective particle

neither more nor less than a descent into hell, a hell that is identical with the world of human existence.[31]

The resemblance of Galatians 3 to Gnostic texts is also illustrated by the appearance of the abstract noun *pístis* ("faith") as a savior figure in vv. 23 and 25.[32] As is usual in Gnosticism, Paul plays on a mixture of the abstract and personal in order to describe the process of revelation and liberation. The identification of *pístis* and *Christós* seems to be clear for the readers; the juxtaposition of *pístis* and *Christós*, however, forces the same readers to reflect on the further relations of what is described. Deliverance from the prison and slavery of sin and law is accomplished through Jesus as a revelation of loyalty.[33]

---

in v. 13 is symptomatic of the function of the entire verse. Verse 13 actually serves as a break from what has just preceded. The introduction of *Christós* at this point jars the memory of the audience back to what has been mentioned in 3:1. There we had the reference to the original message of the Gospel as well as the claim that the opponents had put the Galatians under a spell. The effect of v. 13 is to bring the Galatians up short in their contemplation of the fate awaiting those who would enter the Law."

31. Ibid., 66-67. Dewey here shows that Gal. 3:13 is closely connected with v. 10. Paul continues his discussion of the magical power of the curse. On p. 69, Dewey says: "Paul effects an entirely new reading from Deut. 21:23 by having the oral message of the death of Jesus meet the written curse. The significance of the death of Christ, when placed up against the power and fate of tradition engenders further interpretation. . . . In doing so Paul tries to be even a greater magician than his opponents. For the message itself is powerful, already having produced (*exēgórasen*) what it says."

32. This hypostatization of *pístis* has received far too little attention. That it is not so innocuous is shown not only by the parallelizing of *pístis* with Jesus as a revealer and savior but also by the fact that *pístis* as an hypostasis appears as a revealer and savior in Gnostic texts. This usage is already found in Jewish Gnosticism: Epistle of Eugnostos (III) 78:4; 82:6; 83:1; Paraphrase of Shem (VII) 26:14; 28:30; 30:2, 5, 11, 20; 31:20, 26; 32:11; 33:25; 34:22; 35:11, 27, 33; 37:4; 41:19, 25, 32; 42:8, 11; 43:4, 15; 46:18, 28. In the Apocryphon of John and the tractates on the *Hypostasis of the Archons* and the *Origin of the World*, it appears in passages that have undergone only superficial Christian redaction. Naturally it also appears in the work called Pistis Sophia. The similarity or even identity of *pístis* and *sophía* ("wisdom") is also found in the Epistle of Eugnostos (III) 82:5; 83:1 and the Paraphrase of Shem (VII) 31:26; 33:25; 46:18, 28. Other Jewish Gnostic passages in which *pístis* is not clearly hypostatized include Paraphrase of Shem 25:15; 26:5; 30:29; 34:22; 35:27, 29.

33. Besides the concentration of Gnostic motifs in Gal. 3:10—4:10, the allegory

It is noteworthy that throughout Galatians Paul speaks only of Jesus' coming (incarnation) and crucifixion, never of his resurrection or ascension. Still, Paul clearly conceives of Jesus as being alive and present and makes the ecclesiological dimensions of the Christ figure clear-cut at the end of chap. 3 (3:27: "put on Christ"; 3:28: "one in Christ"; see also 2:17; 3:14). The Jewish Gnostic texts under discussion consistently speak of exaltation and glorification in conjunction with earthly epiphany or descent.[34] In Galatians, on the other hand, Paul restricts himself to Jesus' descent, submission, and death on the cross.[35] Gnosticism opens the way to heaven, but Paul radicalizes the protest of the Gnostic texts against the hegemonic structures and the religion(s) of existing society. This impression is reinforced when one turns to the contrast Paul draws up in 3:19 between the descended Jesus and the figures of angels, and especially Moses, responsible for giving the law. This passage may be compared with the texts cited by Fallon from the tractates (*The nature of the archons* and *On the origin of the world*) out of the Nag Hammadi library from

---

of the two mothers in 4:22-31 bears out the similarity of Paul's argument in Galatians to Gnostic tradition. The implicit motif of the virgin birth appears not only in Philo's description of Sarah and other women (e.g., *Cherubim* 8; 40–52; 59–64; *Leg. All.* 3, 217; *Post.* 134; *Ebr.* 59) but also in the Nag Hammadi texts. There are particularly close parallels in the Apocalypse of Adam (V) 78:18-26; 79:28—80:9; 81:1-14; all in the context of the poetical interpolation. The significant point is not just the parallelism of the individual motifs but also the parallelism of their juxtaposition in both Galatians and the Apocalypse of Adam, above all in the self-contained poetical interpolation. In both Galatians 4 and the Apocalypse of Adam, furthermore, the motif of the virgin birth is followed by mention of the child's persecution (Gal. 4:29; Apoc. of Adam 78:21-23; 79:1-14). The similarity to Revelation 12 suddenly becomes striking. For a discussion of the latter, see Adela Yarbro Collins, *The Combat Myth in the Book of Revelation*, Harvard Dissertations in Religion 9 (Missoula: Scholars Press, 1976).

34. Especially impressive in the poetic description of the thirteen kingdoms in Apoc. of Adam 77:27—82:19. See also Francis T. Fallon, *The Enthronement of Sabaoth: Jewish Elements in Gnostic Creation Myths*, Nag Hammadi Studies 10 (Leiden: E. J. Brill, 1978), esp. 38–61 and 95–111.

35. Paul underscores this theme by repeated reference to being crucified with Jesus (2:19; 5:24; 6:14) and by speaking of Jesus' embodiment in the weak Paul and the weak Galatians (4:14, 19; cf. 6:17).

several other Jewish texts.[36] In these texts, and particularly in their descriptions of Moses, exaltation precedes the giving and receiving of divine revelation.[37]

The Moses of the tradition just discusssed, and of Galatians 3, sets out to ascend the heavenly heights and thus (like other savior figures) reflects the patriarchal image of God the omnipotent king. Paul, on the other hand, sees Jesus, and together with Jesus the one and only God, embarked on the opposite course. This is, to be sure, not a totally new idea; Paul builds on the antimonarchic, democratic tendency already noted as an aspect of Gnosticism. Democratization in Gnosticism, however, usually remains at the level of multiplying the royal and the divine. Paul goes further, questioning the very concepts of monarchy and deity. In this regard, Galatians goes beyond 1 Thessalonians and resembles such texts as Apoc. of Adam 82:19-21, which speaks of a generation without a king, probably the passage's real goal.

What Paul describes in Galatians 3 must have been understood by the ancient world as the overthrow of the gods, including the biblical God. For Paul, incarnation and crucifixion mean a humanization of God. This humanization of God in Jesus continues in incorporation of Jesus' followers (Gal. 3:27: "put on Christ"; 3:18: "one in Christ"). In the accursed Jesus, God's solidarity with those under the curse nullifies the alienation of human beings brought about and maintained by the law, by their division into peoples, classes, and sexes. The congregation of Jesus becomes the exemplary community of those who are set free. As the androgynous dimension of 3:28 suggests, Paul is working in this instance not only with social models but also with the Gnostic transformation of the myth of the primeval human being. This

36. Fallon, *Enthronement of Sabaoth*, 46–54. Fallon also cites the Tragedies of Ezekiel from Eusebius *Praeparatio Evangelica* (ed. Karl Mras, Die griechischen christlichen Schriftsteller der ersten Jahrhunderte 43/1 [Berlin: Akademie-Verlag, 1954]), 529–30; Phil *De Vita Mosis* 1.148–59, 212–13; 2.7, 46–47, 188–92, 288–91; among others.

37. In his exegesis of the two Nag Hammadi texts, Fallon speaks also of exaltation to the role of judge.

Gnostic reading of the myth presents primeval humanity as an alternative utopia (described in religious terms, but with social intentions), a human race characterized not by the alienating constraint of coercion but by freedom and insight.[38] In Gal. 3:28, Paul brings this concept to bear much more directly on the present reality of the human race and its concrete social structures. He radicalizes the Gnostic protest as well as its promise, turning them into an alternative organizational model.

In Gal. 5:11 the phrase *skándalon toū staurou* (scandal of the cross) appears:

> "But my friends, why am I still being persecuted if I am still preaching circumcision? In that case the *skándalon* of the cross has been removed."

This *skándalon* reflects and summarizes the christological discussion in chaps. 2–4.[39] Paul uses it for a concept that must not be relinquished. The *skándalon* does not only exist in the eyes of unbelievers or the Jews. No, the *skándalon* must not be taken away from the proclamation of the gospel itself— it must remain part and parcel of the faith. But Paul does not tell what is meant by this *skándalon.* He does not define the term here, and suggests its content only very tersely by adding "of the cross." The phrase is supposed to summarize Paul's

38. Texts such as the Apocalypse of Adam (81:1–14) use the motif of the androgynous primeval human being as the model of reconciled humanity. But according to Apoc. of Adam 64:6–20, the original human state is also androgynous, and the fall goes hand in hand with the differentiation of the sexes. For a discussion of the whole problem, see Pagels, *The Gnostic Gospels* (New York: Random House, 1979), 48–69; Arthur, *Wisdom Goddess,* passim. See also Wayne Meeks, "The Image of the Androgyne: Some Uses of a Symbol in Earliest Christianity," *Harvard Theological Review* 83: 165–208; see further Dennis R. MacDonald, *There Is No Male and Female,* Harvard Dissertations in Religion 20 (Philadelphia : Fortress Press, 1987).

39. See Gustav Stählin *"skándalon,"* in *TDNT,* 7:339–58, with bibliography. See also Karlheinz Müller, *Anstoss und Gericht: Eine Studie zum jüdischen Hintergrund des paulinischen "skándalon,"-Begriffs,* Studien zum Alten und Neuen Testament 19 (Munich: Kösel-Verlag, 1969).

intention.[40] It is reasonable to assume that *skándalon toū stauroū* is a stereotyped expression since Paul cites it without further exposition. Nowhere else does Paul explain the term *skándalon* either. In part, it is directly dependent on the Septuagint,[41] but Paul's positive use of the word has no parallel there.[42] The theological basis is that Paul—probably following a tradition of the early church[43]—interprets the combination of Isa. 8:14 and 28:16 christologically.[44]

Although Paul never explains *skándalon* directly, he does provide clues in the related terms and antonyms he associates with it. First of all there are the synonyms *pagís* and *théra* ("trap," "snare") in Rom. 11:9, quoting Ps. 69. These synonyms come close to the basic meaning of *skándalon* as "trap." Ps. 69 describes hardness of heart; it also uses *antapódoma* ("retribution"), which looks forward to judgment. Next, in Rom. 9:33 and 14:13, which has been already mentioned, one finds *próskomma*, "stumbling-block," vividly accentuated in 9:33 by the metaphors "stone" and "rock." While 14:13 stands in an ethical context, 9:33 is clearly a christological interpretation, probably based on tradition.[45] The polemical fragment Rom. 16:17-20 uses *dichostasía* ("dissensions") as a synonym for *skándalon.* The two terms together describe the disturbance caused by those who teach falsely. In another polemical passage, 1 Cor. 1:22-24, *skándalon* is associated with the terms *mōría* ("folly"), *sēmeîon* ("sign"), and *dýnamis* ("power").

40. This point must be made over against Heinz Wolfgang Kuhn, who ignores it in his article "Jesus als Gekreuzigter in der frühchristlichen Verkündigung bis zur Mitte des 2. Jahrhunderts," *Zeitschrift für Theologie und Kirche* 72 (1975): 1–46.

41. Rom. 9:33; 11:9. The same pair of terms appears in both Rom. 9:33 and 14:13.

42. The Septuagint uses the noun and the verb in the active voice only in a negative sense; see Stählin, *"skándalon,"* 341–43.

43. To that end see the same combination with a similar interpretation in 1 Pet. 2:6-8.

44. Galatians antedates this interpretation in Rom. 9:33, but the evidence cited in the previous note argues for an early Christian tradition.

45. See n. 108 above.

The meaning of *skándalon* for Paul is to be sought where these terms overlap.[46] The translation "offence" will not suffice. One must also take into account the term's association with "signs and wonders" as well as "wisdom and folly," and give full weight to the ambivalence of Pauline usage, which verges on dialectic. Finally, the polemical passages[47] suggest the dimension of something at once forbidden and fascinating.[48]

Now Galatians—not least in its polemic—deals with satanic charms and enchantment. But it also, in conscious and complex dialectic, deals with divine countercharms. It is therefore reasonable to ask whether the term *skándalon* in Galatians 5 and 1 Corinthians may not also have something to do with magic.[49] The solution to the riddle is to be sought in what Stählin has described as an aspect of *skándalon* in vulgar usage: there it refers to entertainment, especially acrobatics—and specifically juggling.[50]

46. Recognizing the positive sense of *skándalon* in Gal. 5:11 and following the lead of K. Müller, Kuhn ("Jesus als Gekreuzigter," 36) has suggested understanding the word as "Anstoss." In proposing this, he is guided by the peculiar ambivalence of this German word which has a positive as well as a negative sense. "Anstoss" in German can mean both "(cause of) offense" and "incitement." The actual ambiguity of this term in German has misled Kuhn into seeing the same ambiguity in the Greek term *skándalon*. Paul, however, could not have used such an equivocation, because the Greek word does not share the same ambiguity. The very real conceptual ambivalence must be represented by other translations more appropriate to the semantic field of the Greek.

47. As well as the biblical association with idols; Stählin, "*skándalon*," 343.

48. This aspect, even while voicing sharp criticism, nevertheless presupposes a common set of criteria.

49. The word's history suggests the meaning "jugglery," which also includes the connotations entrapment, deception, trickery, and fraud. But the translation "jugglery" would be too negative; it is not dialectical enough to comprehend the full semantic range of the Pauline term. On the other hand, the translation "enchantment" might have too positive a ring to it.

50. A derivative *skandalistēs*, which Otto Stählin translates "acrobat," appears in a second-century C.E. inscription from Delphi (see Wilhelm Dittenberger, *Sylloge Inscriptionum Graecarum*, 3d ed. [Leipzig: Hirzel, 1915-24], 847.5). Wilhelm Kroll, "*skandalistēs*," *PW*, 3A:438, prefers the translation "magician." Compare Stählin, "*skándalon*," 339, n. 8. This derivative presupposes not only a corresponding professional activity with some history behind it but also an ongoing use of *skándalon* to describe the activity.

But there is still more to say concerning both Gal. 5:11 and 1 Cor. 1:23 and their respective contexts. Both passages suggest that there are ramifications in the field of the word *skándalon* which for Paul relate to Christology and anthropology, and the understanding of office associated with them. The context of Gal. 5:11 is a bitterly sarcastic polemic which reaches its climax (5:12) in a vulgar pun that refers obscenely to circumcision/cutting around: "I wish they would cut off/ castrate themselves"—in other words, Paul wishes that the knife would slip and castrate those who perform the rite of circumcision on others.[51] Once alerted to the strained humor of the passage, one detects yet another ironic implication. The question introducing 5:11 implies that circumcision and persecution, or even the preaching of circumcision, and the *skándalon toū stauroū* are mutually exclusive. One would think that circumcision itself would be a *skándalon* in Jewish eyes, a confession of faith and a source of mockery as well as danger for those who are circumcised.[52] Thus to Jewish readers Paul's imputations concerning circumcision are a cruel joke, a malicious burlesque not only of their customs and ideas but also of their religious history, which Paul shares.

But coarse or even vulgar humor used in polemic to caricature hallowed traditions was a common feature of the diatribe used by popular philosophy, and especially in mime, the street theater of the ancient world. The Jews, too, were

51. Paul makes a similar vulgar joke in Phil. 3:2, where he pretends a slip of the pen makes him write *katatomē* (abscission) instead of *peritomē* (circumcision). See Hans von Campenhausen, "Ein Witz des Apostels Paulus und die Anfänge des christlichen Humors," *Neutestamentliche Studien für Rudolf Bultmann zum 70. Geburtstag,* Beihefte zur Zeitschrift für die Neutestamentliche Wissenschaft (Berlin: Töpelmann, 1954), 189-93. Of course Paul has much more to contribute to the theme of humor than this bad joke, which moreover has different overtones in the mouth of someone who is not Jewish than in the mouth of the Jewish author, who, being circumcised himself, is engaging in self-irony. This would not hold true for a Gentile except in countries like the United States where all males are regularly circumcised.
52. In the period of Antiochus IV, circumcision was grounds for persecution. Later, Jews were scorned and ridiculed for this religious "disfigurement," which in turn was reinforced as a confessional mark of distinctiveness. The general practice of bodily mutilation in honor of the deity is discussed below (pp. 79-80).

familiar with persiflage and even parody from the biblical tradition, especially the prophets.[53] In Deutero-Isaiah, at the latest, burlesque and parody became instruments of prophetic revelation.[54] Under the influence of Deutero-Isaiah, the three latest offshoots of the wisdom movement (missionary, apocalyptic, and Gnostic wisdom) made increasing use of caricature and travesty. From the time of the Wisdom of Solomon on,[55] these stylistic features became essential elements of Gnostic revelation. The emphasis on the dramatic aspect of the artificial mythicizing, characteristic for Gnosticism, shows that there was more stylistic borrowing from the mime than from the diatribe.[56]

Elements of persiflage, perhaps even of parody and burlesque, appear in Galatians even before chap. 5, namely in 1:8-9; 2:4, 6; 3:1-5, 13, 19, 23-25; 4:1-10, 13-20. Initially they are associated chiefly with negative polemic. From 3:13 on, however, one also finds parody used paradoxically in a positive sense to reveal a christological and soteriological truth.[57] The polemical and parodistic style of the epistle already makes it appear highly aggressive; this effect is strengthened by the dramatic flair produced by the strikingly mythical sections of chaps. 3 and 4. Once again, in these chapters the mime is a more likely influence than the diatribe.[58]

Because today we think of Galatians as a sacred text, centuries old, we can hardly imagine the shocking effect it

53. The story of the golden calf (Exodus 32) is a particularly clever parody.

54. See esp. Isaiah 40; 44; 47; 54.

55. Not just in Wisdom of Soloman 13; 14, a burlesque of idolatry echoing Deutero-Isaiah, but above all in the wonderful parodies in chaps. 2 (including 1:16 and 3:1-9); 5; and 17–18.

56. On this point, the remarks of mine on the Wisdom of Solomon in my annotated translation and in my article "Wesen der Wahrheit" need to be expanded substantially.

57. One finds ironic comparison of curse to revelation, subjugation, imprisonment, and enslavement to redemption and liberation. The comparison of *nómos* ("law") to *pístis* ("faith") must also have struck the ancient reader as comical or satirical.

58. See Thomas Gelzer and H. Marti, "Mimos/Mimus," in *Lexikon der Alten Welt* (Zurich: Ariemis, 1965), cols. 1962–63; also Karl Vretska, "Mimos," in *Der kleine Pauly* (Stuttgart: Druckenmüller, 1964), vol. 3, cols. 1309–14.

had on its first readers. Christian apologetics, the Constantinian settlement, and above all Protestant orthodoxy have disaccustomed us to the positive potential and possibilities of burlesque and parody. These possibilities, from both the Bible and the contemporary world, were familiar to Paul's original readers. In particular, they knew that one's own familiar and therefore sacred tradition may be parodied or mocked, that sacred cows may be lampooned, for the sake of new or better insights.

The victorious element of the church later curried favor with the Roman authorities by claiming to support the state. They proved this claim not least by giving up the church's originally very strong association with diatribe and mime. With this, the church triumphant lost its essential instruments of social and political criticism. The state, after all, was increasingly deifying itself, and deemed such instruments of criticism as corrupting. A state that considers itself absolute must see any parody of itself and of law, order, and the official religion as destructive of its authority. A religion that supports the state as representing the divine order on earth cannot tolerate the idea of burlesquing the divine—not to mention the notion that God might burlesque himself and his representatives. But this is the very point of the *skándalon toū stauroū*. What is under attack is not just Jewish legalism but the very foundations of Hellenistic society. The humor of the Bible, and especially of the New Testament, is incompatible with reverence for a sanctity and majesty that support the power of the establishment.

It would be wrong to understand this criticism as withdrawal from the world and its political life. Not only the end of chap. 3 and the beginning of chap. 4 but also the parenesis in chaps. 5 and 6 show that Galatians develops a concrete alternative social utopia. This alternative utopia incorporates several central ideals of Hellenistic society—in particular its libertarian and democratic universalism,[59] its socially egalitarian pluralism,[60] and its urban basis.[61] But Paul is convinced

59. The church embracing both Jews and Gentiles and its world mission.

that realization of this utopia requires a fundamental reorientation—already begun in the revelation of Christ—that extends to the realities of authority and sacredness.

First Corinthians:
The Corporate Identity of the Christ

In 1 Corinthians, Paul pursues this critical approach that caricatures not only the religiosity of the day but also the ideology sustaining the social and political order. Here Paul professedly draws on the dialectic shaped by the experience and thought of the wisdom tradition, above all in its radically dualistic Gnostic form. He expresses this dialectic with a christological energy that surpasses what is found in Galatians. In 1 Cor. 1:18—2:9, Paul uses a mimetic parody of the wisdom myth[62] to describe the historical crucifixion of Jesus as the revelation of God's essential nature.[63]

---

60. The description of the church's unity at the end of chap. 3.

61. The resolution proposed by the Jerusalem conference in Gal. 2:9-11 transposes to the church of Jesus Christ the structure of the Hellenistic city as a collection of various *politeúmata*, each with its own affiliations and loyalties extending beyond the boundaries of the particular city.

62. For a discussion of the wisdom background of 1 Cor. 1:17—2:16, see Conzelmann, *1 Corinthians* (Philadelphia: Fortress Press, 1975), 39–69. Conzelmann rightly stresses the speculative character of Paul's wisdom background, see 43–46, 56–61, 65–67. My study of the wisdom literature of biblical Judaism has convinced me that in 1 Corinthians Paul is drawing particularly on the Gnostic form of wisdom, with its special emphasis on, and fondness for, parodistic dualism.

63. Here the term *skándalon* appears once more. In contrast to Gal. 5:11, it is used negatively and limited to the Jews. It would be a mistake, however, to conclude that one is dealing here with an ethnic, subjectivizing restriction of the term, that it refers only to the judgment facing the Jews and no longer possesses an inherent dimension of revelation. There is still the association with the cross, as well as the use of the synonym *mōría* ("folly"). Since in the ensuing discussion, despite the association of strength and wisdom with the revelation of God, weakness and folly

[18]For the word of the cross is folly to those who are perishing, but to us who are being saved it is the power of God. [19]For it is written,

"I will destroy the wisdom of the wise,

and the cleverness of the clever I will thwart."

[20]Where is the one who is wise? Where is the scribe? Where is the debater of this age? Has not God made foolish the wisdom of the world? [21]For since, in the wisdom of God, the world did not know God through wisdom, it pleased God through the folly of what we preach to save those who believe. [22]For Jews demand signs and Greeks seek wisdom, [23] but we preach Christ crucified, a stumbling block to Jews and folly to Gentiles, [24]but to those who are called, both Jews and Greeks, Christ the power of God and the wisdom of God. [25]For God's foolishness is wiser than human wisdom, and God's weakness is stronger than human strength.

[26]For consider your call, brothers and sisters; not many of you were wise according to worldly standards, not many were powerful, not many were of noble birth; [27]but God chose what is foolish in the world to shame the wise, God chose what is weak in the world to shame the strong. [28] God chose what is low and despised in the world, even things that are not, to bring to nothing things that are, [29]so that no human being might boast in the presence of God. [30]He is the source of your life in Christ Jesus, whom God made our wisdom, our righteousness and sanctification and redemption; [31]therefore, as it is written, "Let the one who boasts, boast of the Lord."

[2:1]When I came to you, brothers and sisters, I did not come proclaiming to you the testimony of God in

---

are also ranged on the positive side, one must conclude (in the absence of any explicit statement) that the same is true of *skándalon.* This conclusion is confirmed by 1 Cor. 2:1-5. There, too, the dialectic does not nullify the fact that Paul appears as a weak figure, fearful, hesitant, and without plausible words of wisdom. The demonstration of the Spirit and power is, therefore, linked to such weakness and does not make its appearance otherwise.

lofty words or wisdom. [2]For I decided to know nothing among you except Jesus Christ and him crucified. [3]And I was with you in weakness and in much fear and trembling; [4]and my speech and my message were not in plausible words of wisdom, but in demonstration of the Spirit and of power, [5]that your faith might not rest in human wisdom but in the power of God.

[6]Yet among the mature we do impart wisdom, although it is not a wisdom of this age or of the rulers of this age, who are doomed to pass away. [7]But we impart a secret and hidden wisdom of God, which God decreed before the ages for our glorification. [8]None of the rulers of this age understood this; for if they had, they would not have crucified the Lord of glory. [9]But, as it is written,

"What no eye has seen, nor ear heard,

nor the human heart conceived,

what God has prepared for those who love him,"
[10]God has revealed to us through the Spirit.

This presentation of the crucifixion abrogates not only the Gnostic understanding of revelation, which is antihistorical, but also the predominant religious and inter-cultural identification of wisdom with the divine and folly with the human. Confession to Jesus as the sign of God's decisive act stands God on the head. It does the same to all forms of power and authority, not just religious—although in the ancient world religious authority was the wellspring and symbol of all social control and political authority and might.

The parody of the divine epiphany in 1 Cor. 1:18-25 has its counterpart (characteristic of the mime) in the unvarnished description of the audience in 1:26-29: the common people were the milieu of Hellenistic street theater. Their lives were imitated, and the parodies of the gods were related to them. Paul does the same thing. Social realism corresponds to the

realism of theological critique. Social realism was still considered vulgar in the Hellenistic world.[64] Paul maintains this
vulgarity in 1 Corinthians.[65]

64. This attitude is demonstrated even by Petronius's *Satyricon*. With regard to
the social setting of the Corinthian congregation, I cannot agree with Wuellner's
objections to a realistic interpretation of these verses (Wilhelm Wuellner, "The Sociological Implications of I Corinthians 1:26-28 Reconsidered," in *Studia Evangelica*
4, Texte und Untersuchungen 112 [Berlin: Walter de Gruyter, 1973], 666–72). His
stylistic arguments are not persuasive. Wuellner even proposes the opposite theory,
namely that the Corinthian congregation recruited its members primarily from among
the prosperous, bourgeois middle class, together with a certain percentage from the
upper class and a few of the very poor. A similar hypothesis was proposed earlier
by E. A. Judge, *The Social Pattern of Christian Groups in the First Century* (London:
Tyndale Press, 1960).

Theissen has presented a much more nuanced picture of the Corinthian congregation's social structure. See Gerd Theissen, "Social Stratification in the Corinthian
Community," 231–71; and idem, "The Strong and Weak in Corinth," 272–89; both in
The Social Setting of Pauline Christianity (Philadelphia: Fortress Press, 1982). He
finds in the congregation people of relatively high social status with substantial
income or property, but they constitute a minority, albeit an influential one. Theissen's
theory is accepted with some modifications by Abraham Malherbe, *Social Aspects
of Early Christianity*, 2d ed. (Philadelphia: Fortress Press, 1983), 71–91.

While it is clear that the congregation included persons of considerable means,
it is equally obvious that 1 Corinthians does not discuss the specific problems of
their class or professions. The contrast between the Corinthian correspondence and
the Pastorals, which date from the second century, abundantly illustrates the values
of "bourgeois Christianity" found in the latter. Nothing of this sort is found in
1 Corinthians.

65. Note both the description of Paul's appearance at Corinth in 2:1-5, which
must have struck Hellenistic eyes and ears as a virtual caricature, and Paul's extreme
description of himself in chap. 4, esp. 4:11-13. The subject matter and style of the
discussions in chaps. 6 and 7, too, would have seemed "common" to the elevated
taste of the ancient world. The debates about meat offered to idols, wearing veils,
and the Lord's Supper are likewise not aimed at the "elevated" reader. Chapter 13
celebrates love as *agápē*, a word that for cultured listeners would have a pedestrian,
probably even vulgar and lewd, connotation. Furthermore, it is rarely noted that in
this chapter Paul generally avoids using any terms that are exclusively religious;
those that do appear (vv. 1-3) are treated negatively. Neither God nor Christ is mentioned in this extremely "secular" chapter. This "profanation" is undoubtedly inten-
tional. The format for worship that Paul recommends in chap. 14 must have seemed
even more chaotic to Romans in Corinth, especially the educated, than to Greeks.
The claim that the physical body is resurrected must have appeared totally crude
and tasteless. Paul's Corinthian congregation is a far cry from being a religious
organization serving the Greek or Roman middle class. The catechumens and members belonging to these circles must be considered social mavericks.

These observations cast a special light on 1 Cor. 2:8. The "rulers of this age" who "did not understand wisdom" and "crucified the Lord of glory" are surely mythological powers, not earthly figures.[66] It is appropriate to the parodistic style that has taken over in 1:18 for Paul to employ in 2:8 the Gnostic motif of deceiving the demons. This motif appears already in Wisd. of Sol., chapters 1–5, 17, and 18, where not only fools are deceived by God, Wisdom, and Wisdom's agent, but also the powers associated with or controlling them.[67] Paul radicalizes the dialectic of this basically docetic understanding of revelation[68] by introducing the crucifixion of the human person Jesus, referring to him—with an emphasis unusual for Paul—as the "Lord of glory." In the face of a theology that turns its back on the world of history, Paul insists on the crucifixion of Jesus as the decisive demonstration of God's glory and rulership.[69]

Taken with a grain of salt, what Paul says in 1 Cor. 2:8 about true rule, and what he says against the demonic powers,

66. This was first pointed out by Martin Dibelius, *Die Geisterwelt im Glauben des Paulus* (Göttingen: Vandenhoeck & Ruprecht, 1909), 92ff. See also Hans von Campenhausen, "Zur Auslegung von Röm 13: die dämonistische Deutung des EXOΘΣIA Begriffs," *Festschrift für Alfred Bertholetzum 80. Geburtstag* (Tübingen: Mohr, 1950), 97–113. Miller's attempted return to a historical interpretation (Gene Miller, "AΠXONTΩN TOY AIΩNOΣ TOYTOY: A New Look at 1 Corinthians 2:6-8," *Journal of Biblical Literature* 91 [1972], 522–28) is not convincing; he does not take the counterarguments of Dibelius and others seriously enough.

67. In this theme, Gnosticism borrowed a burlesque motif from the realm of folk-lore (deception of the evil demon or devil) and gave it a central position in its understanding of revelation. The mime probably helped this development. Lührmann's misgivings (*Offenbarungsverständnis bei Paulus und in paulinischen Gemeinden*, Wissenschaftliche Mongraphien zum Alten und Neuen Testament 16 [Neukirchen: Neukirchener Verlag, 1965], 137) as to the use of the Gnostic myth are met by noting the essential revelatory dimensions of the myth as well as the possibility that wisdom may have multiple embodiments.

68. See Dieter Georgi, "Weisheit Salomos," in *Jüdische Schriften aus hellenistisch-römischer Zeit,* ed. Werner Georg Kümmel (Gütersloh: Mohn, 1980), 3: 402–19.

69. I cannot understand why Lührmann (*Offenbarungsverständnis*, 137) says: "Neither the cross nor the 'historical Jesus' represents revelation to Paul." Already in the Wisdom of Solomon the embodiment of wisdom in the sage is revelation, necessarily paradoxical and dialectical. For Paul hidenness is even more central to the nature of revelation.

reflects on the nature of all established rulership: it is incompatible with authentic rulership as revealed in Jesus. By comparison, it is ridiculous, ineffectual, illusory. Authentic rule does not establish its abode on high but in the depths. It is hidden, not open, and precisely for that reason effectual.

In the remainder of 1 Corinthians, Paul goes on to discuss this christologized theology at greater length in the context of a discussion concerning the life of the community. Paul understands the local congregation literally as an assembly of the people (*ekklēsía*). This word does not appear as a technical term in the Greek of the Jewish Bible or of the Jewish community; neither is it typically religious. It was very familiar, however, in the local political life of the Hellenistic city. Paul chose it to indicate that the assembly of those who followed Jesus, the assembly called together in a particular city in the name of the biblical God, was in competition with the local political assembly of the citizenry, the official *ekklēsía*.[70] The world is meant to hear the claim that the congregation of Jesus, gathered in the name of the God of the Bible, is where the interests of the city in question truly find expression.[71]

70. The occasion and conduct of such an *ekklēsía*, held in the local theater, is described vividly by Luke in Acts 19:23-41. In my opinion, Schrage has demonstrated impressively (Wolfgang Schrage, " 'Ekklesia' und 'Synagoge': Zum Ursprung des urchristlichen Kirchenbegriffs," *Zeitschrift für Theologie und Kirche* 60 [1963]: 180–86; see also idem, "synagōgé," in *TDNT*, 7:798–852, esp. 828–29) that the choice of *ekklēsía* to describe the Jesus-congregation(s) was not determined by the usage of the Septuagint. Schrage's explanation that the early church chose *ekklēsía* instead of *synagōgé* to emphasize its distinctiveness from the synagogue, however, is not persuasive. On the one hand, evidence for such a calculated distinction before the First Jewish War is hard to find; on the other, the term "synagogue" continues to appear in Christian usage during the second century, even in the works of the highly anti-Jewish apologists—in other words, at a time when the separation of Christianity from Judaism was already well advanced.

71. One could argue contrariwise that the *ekklēsía* of Jesus is not only the local assembly of Jesus: each individual congregation—in Corinth, Thessalonica, or wherever—represents the universal *ekklēsía theoū* locally, at least according to the introductions of Paul's letters. But this notion of representation, which is shared by the groups devoted to the mysteries, also describes how the individual Hellenistic cities thought of themselves (though they do not use this terminology). They claimed to represent not merely their local city but the totality of Hellenistic civilization, each

This concrete political concern also appears in chap. 12.

> Now concerning spiritual gifts, brothers and sisters,
> I do not want you to be uninformed. [2]You know that
> when you were heathen, you were led astray to dumb
> idols, however you may have been moved. [3]Therefore
> I want you to understand that no one speaking by the
> Spirit of God ever says "Jesus be cursed!" and no one
> can say "Jesus is Lord" except by the Holy Spirit.
> [4]Now there are varieties of gifts, but the same
> Spirit; [5]and there are varieties of service, but the same
> Lord; [6]and there are varieties of working, but it is the
> same God who inspires them all in every one. [7]To each
> is given the manifestation of the Spirit for the common
> good. [8]To one is given through the Spirit the utterance
> of wisdom, and to another the utterance of knowledge
> according to the same Spirit, [9]to another faith by the
> same Spirit, to another gifts of healing by the one Spirit,
> [10]to another the working of miracles, to another proph-
> ecy, to another the ability to distinguish between spirits,
> to another various kinds of tongues, to another the
> interpretation of tongues. [11]All these are inspired by
> one and the same Spirit, who apportions to each one
> individually as the Spirit wills.
> [12]For just as the body is one and has many mem-
> bers, and all the members of the body, though many,
> are one body, so it is with Christ. [13]For by one Spirit
> we were all baptized into one body—Jews or Greeks,
> slave or free—and all were made to drink of one Spirit.
> [14]For the body does not consist of one member
> but of many. [15]If the foot should say, "Because I am not
> a hand, I do not belong to the body," that would not
> make it any less a part of the body. [16]And if the ear

---

city better than all the rest. This chauvinism of the individual cities is manifested,
for example, in a frenzy of architectural activities that sometimes bordered the
grotesque.

should say, "Because I am not an eye, I do not belong to the body," that would not make it any less a part of the body. [17]If the whole body were an eye, where would be the hearing? If the whole body were an ear, where would be the sense of smell? [18]But as it is, God arranged the organs in the body, each one of them, as he chose. [19]If all were a single organ, where would the body be? [20]As it is, there are many parts, yet one body. [21]The eye cannot say to the hand, "I have no need of you," nor again the head to the feet, "I have no need of you." [22]On the contrary, the parts of the body which seem to be weaker are indispensable, [23]and those parts of the body which we think less honorable we invest with the greater honor, and our unpresentable parts are treated with greater modesty, [24]which our more presentable parts do not require. But God has so composed the body, giving the greater honor to the inferior part, [25]that there may be no discord in the body, but that the members may have the same care for one another. [26]If one member suffers, all suffer together; if one member is honored, all rejoice together. [27]Now you are the body of Christ and individually members of it.

Here Paul concludes the eminently praxis-oriented discussions of 1 Corinthians with an investigation into the concrete character of the community. This community is based on the participatory democracy that he understands as the body of Christ. In 12:1-10 he shows that the body of Christ is a pluralistic and egalitarian entity. In it unity and diversity stand in dialectical relationship, and all of the members have equal rights. Not even Christ is superior (as head, say); rather Christ is identical with the community at large (1 Cor. 12:12). Thus not only unity but also authority find expression in pluralism.

The reader will find a marked difference between the distinctly mythical description in 12:1-13, especially 12-13, and the more metaphoric and organic description of the *sōma* in 12:14-27. The latter interprets the former. While the mythicizing description builds on the Gnostic myth,[72] the metaphoric and organic discussion draws on Hellenistic and Roman political philosophy.[73] Paul modifies the motif of the transpersonal body by treating it not only as an inclusive mythical entity but also as an active collective community consciousness in the form of pluralistic responsibility and participation.

The Pauline version of the body motif involves none of the hierarchical structures so highly developed in the political version of this symbol, most notably in its Roman dress. The latter posits a microcosm-macrocosm correlation between the individual, the state bureaucracy or society, and the universe; in any given period, the "head," the Caesar, represents the correlation in a very special way. Besides exercising sovereignty, he represents the unity and authenticity of society and cosmos. He simultaneously personifies the chief of state and the deity who governs the world. In interrelating God, Christ, human life, and human community (the *ekklesia*) as Christ's bodily identity, Paul (in 1 Corinthians) brings this political symbolism down to earth—literally turning the body symbol on its head. In doing so he produces a coarse joke, equally political as religious.

The political and organizational ideologies contemporary with Paul aimed at "order" (*táxis, ordo*). It is therefore all the more remarkable that Paul does not try to organize the truly

72. The Gnostic understanding of *sōma* ("body") in the New Testament period has been reexamined by Egon Brandenburger, *Adam und Christus: Exegetisch-religionsgeschichtliche Untersuchungen zu Römer 5,12-21 (1. Kor. 15)*, Wissenschaftliche Monographien zum Alten und Neuen Testament 7 (Neukirchen: Neukirchener Verlag, 1962), esp. 119–31, and idem, *Fleisch und Geist: Paulus und die dualistische Weisheit*, Wissenschaftliche Monographien zum Alten und Neuen Testament 29 (Neukirchen: Neukirchener Verlag, 1968), esp. 197–216. Brandenburger uses terminology like "Heilsraum" ("the space or sphere of salvation").

The studies of Brandenburger break through the conceptual Platonism of many articles in TDNT which confuse the lexical occurrence of a term with the historical reality of its meaning. For such Platonism, if the term does not exist, then the subject matter to which the term relates does not exist either.

73. Eduard Schweizer, *sōma* in *TDNT*, 7:1024–94, esp. 1032–41.

tumultuous worship of the Corinthians more rigidly in 1 Cor. 14. He even rejects the organizational model of the local Gnostics. Their elitist emphasis on speaking in tongues could check and control activities indeed, because it allowed only a handful of people—and these the spiritual elite—to speak. Instead, Paul submits a solution that must seem like trying to square the circle: he would structure the event by encouraging everyone to participate as actively as possible, subject only to pragmatic guidelines (14:26-33a).

In this proposal, Paul advocates an enormous expansion of the function which, in the political sphere, both biblical and pagan tradition had staunchly restricted to an elite—namely prophecy. In the ancient world, prophets[74] played an extraordinarily vital role with respect to society: they mediated between God and humanity. Their status in the biblical tradition was even higher, because they were looked upon as central members of the heavenly court (1 Kings 22:19-28; Isa. 6; Zech. 3).

In 1 Cor. 14:33, Paul says: "God is not a God of disorder but of peace." He does not say: "God is not a God of unrest [destabilization] but of order." The ancient ideologies of governance would lead us to expect the latter. The entire Hellenistic world, the Jews included, considered the primary aim of social and political structures to be *táxis* (order), even in the realm of ecstatic prophecy. The majority of Hellenistic readers would express the conviction that peace results from and depends on order.

Second Corinthians: The Secrets of Power

In the fragments of 2 Corinthians,[75] Paul continues to articulate the organizational ideas of 1 Corinthians. It has already been

---

74. For a more detailed discussion of the prophetic role, see Helmut Krämer et al., "*prophḗtēs*," in *TDNT*, 6:828–61.

75. See Günther Bornkamm, *Die Vorgeschichte des sogenannten Zweiten Korintherbriefes*, Sitzungsberichte der Akademie der Wissenschaften, Phil.-hist. Klasse, 1961/2 (Heidelberg: Winter, 1961); Dieter Georgi, *The Opponents of Paul in Second Corinthians* (Philadelphia: Fortress Press, 1986), passim, 9–25, 325–42, 351–58.

noted that Paul does not meet challenges to his authority as an apostle by moving in the opposite direction, toward authoritarianism. Nor does he apply an authoritarian hand to the "aberratians" of ecstatic tumult. Avoiding centralized control, he beats his missionary opponents at their own game, as it were. When Paul wrote the first fragments of 2 Corinthians (2:14—7:4, with the exception of 6:14—7:1) and then shortly thereafter the so-called "sorrowful letter" (chaps. 10–13), he was in an even more desperate situation than during the composition of 1 Corinthians. His authority and leadership were being radically impugned, as well as the theology and Christology on which they were based. It was a textbook situation for vigorous intervention, at least until "normalcy" was restored. But no such intervention takes place. Instead one finds the diametrical opposite: a self-deprecating confession of weakness is the apostle's response when driven into a corner.[76]

Paul's opponents in 2 Corinthians rallied to the flag of victory in religious competition.[77] The critical elements in this competition were personal spiritual exploits, the importance of which the tradition represented: in other words, the achievements of the heroes of the past who were "present" in this tradition. The theory and practice of Paul's opponents correspond to Jewish missionary theology, of which they are a Jesus-oriented version. Jesus is presented as the most important representative of the chain of Jewish tradition, the most miraculous and successful competitor in the contest of religious offerings—those centering on Jesus as well as other Jewish and Gentile claims.

Paul was faced with a group of people who honored themselves as *theîoi* and who honored their hero Jesus as one *theîos ánthropos* ("divine" human). They had successfully adopted the central principles and standards of Hellenistic society, a culture of competition based on meritocracy and a

76. Even the threats to demonstrate strength in 10:6; 12:14; 12:21—13:4; 13:10 are not without dialectical irony.
77. Georgi, *Opponents*, passim.

free market,[78] which felt that these very principles made it democratic.[79] It was a culture of the extraordinary. Amazement (and hence admiration) was the goal and driving force of social aspiration and experience. At the same time there was a slighting of the boundary that separates the human from the divine—in fact the superhuman was taken as the cultural standard. In this society, admiration, esteem, and recognition were crucial motivating factors.[80] Worship of the *princeps*— the Caesar religion—was its capstone, not just politically or religiously, but also economically. The Caesar religion served both as symptom and as stimulus of the economy of the first century. Capitalism became a form of realized eschatology with the supreme capitalist as divine profiteer, provider, and *princeps*.

The christological theology developed by Paul in the fragments of 2 Corinthians stresses even more than his extant earlier writings that the "normal" structures of reality based on demonstration and imposition of power run counter to reality and are in fact destructive.[81] Neither divine nor human reality rests upon them. Only what is weak deserves to be called strong. Only powerlessness is power. This is the special

78. On the social milieu of the *theîos ánthropos* concept, see Dieter Georgi, "Socio-Economic Reasons for the 'Divine Man' as a Propagandistic Pattern," in Aspects of Religious Propoganda in Judaism and Early Christianity, ed. Elisabeth Schüssler Fiorenza idem, (Notre Dame: University of Notre Dame Press, 1967), 27–42; idem, and the epilogue to *Opponents*, 390–422. The latter also discusses the significance of the concept of tradition in ancient society.

79. See also the discussion of democracy above, pp. 12–13.

80. Hellenistic civilization is a miracle-culture. Countless sculptures and inscriptions, especially expressions of gratitude, as well as literary compositions of the period, attest to the performance and experience of extraordinary deeds that engender bewilderment, astonishment, and amazement as well as admiration. The ubiquitous inscriptions voice gratitude for the experience of the divine. Both elements—the experience of these favors and gratitude for them—are important stimuli for the society in all of its sectors, not only the religious and cultural but also the economic and political. Miracles and miracle tales associated with Jesus' followers as well as with Jesus himself are supposed to make the Jesus-communities conform socially.

81. See, e.g., the very fundamental discussion in 2 Cor. 3:6-18, which continues and develops the ideas of Galatians 3 about the law and especially the relationship between letter and spirit; see also 2 Cor. 4:3-6.

theme of the fool's speech in 2 Cor. 11–12. Paul's talent for parody, already observed in Galatians and 1 Corinthians, finds skillful expression here.[82] But Paul does more than simply make himself out to be a fool: behind the *hypèr egō* ("I am a better one") of 2 Cor. 11:23, one catches a glimpse of the face of Jesus himself.[83]

The forms Paul uses in the fragments of 2 Corinthians as well as his polemic indicate that the horizon of his discourse extends beyond personal religion. Under discussion are those who organize the congregations, the structure of these congregations, and their relationships with each other throughout the world.[84] A web of associations and references to the social setting, its structures and centers of power, is thus revealed in the fragments of 2 Corinthians. But this broader world is also addressed directly. This is even truer in 5:14-21 than it is in 3:5—4:6. 2 Corinthians 5:14-21 is concerned not just with the followers of Jesus but with all—that is, all people, the whole world.[85]

> [14]For the love of Christ controls us, because we
> are convinced that one has died for all; therefore all

82. For a discussion of this section, see Georgi, the epilogue of *Opponents*, 337, with additional bibliography. Betz (Hans Dieter Betz, "Eine Christus-Aretalogie bei Paulus," *Zeitschrift für Theologie und Kirche* 66 [1969]: 288–305) provides an excellent analysis of the parodistic nature of this text, which entails a kind of miracle story composed, as it were, "against the grain." The apostle Paul is not hero but *Schweik*, a paradigm for Hasek and Chaplin.

83. See also the phrase *hypèr Christoū* in 2 Cor. 12:10.

84. This is even truer in the chapters that deal with the collection. I discuss their universal aspect in Dieter Georgi, *Remembering the Poor* (Decatur: Abingdon Press, forthcoming). On the basis of a text from Philo, I discuss the relationships, on both the personal and global level, between (*dikaiosýnē* ["justice"]), *isótēs* ("equality"), and *eucharistía* ("gratitude"). These relationships are important not only for Paul but even more so for his Hellenistic environment.

85. The proposition stated in v. 14 is intended in a general and inclusive sense. This dimension of comprehensiveness is maintained in v. 15; there is no trace of any restriction. Verse 19 likewise speaks of the death of Jesus as embracing everyone and everything, the whole world. The parallelism between vv. 19 and 18 raises the question whether the "we" of v. 18 is not also meant to be synonymous with the "world," i.e., "all of us." This question can be extended to v. 21: since in the first half, as in vv. 14 and 15 (as well as vv. 18 and 19), "for our sakes" refers to all humanity, the same is very likely true of "we" in the second half.

have died. [15]And he died for all, that those who live might live no longer for themselves but for him who for their sake died and was raised.

[16]From now on, therefore, we regard no one from a human point of view; even though we once regarded Christ from a human point of view, we regard him thus no longer. [17]Therefore, if any one is in Christ, there is a new creation; the old has passed away, behold, the new has come. [18]All this is from God, who through Christ reconciled us to himself and gave us the ministry of reconciliation; [19]that is, in Christ God was reconciling the world to himself, not counting their trespasses against them, and entrusting to us the message of reconciliation. [20]So we are ambassadors for Christ, God making his appeal through us. We beseech you on behalf of Christ, be reconciled to God. [21]For our sake he made him to be sin who knew no sin, so that in him we might become the righteousness of God.

The propaganda concerning universal reconciliation that originated in the period of Alexander the Great and flared up once more in the first century B.C.E. reappears here. Käsemann[86] has suggested that in 5:19-21 Paul is drawing upon a Jewish Christian hymnic tradition. It seems to me that the panegyric tone is explained sufficiently by the observation that here—not only in v. 19, but also already in v. 14—Paul is employing and modifying the propagandistic language of political theology with its ideology of reconciliation and peace.

The best example is Plutarch's *De Alexandri magni fortuna aut virtute* (329 C):

> "But [Alexander] thought that he had come as both a unifier and a reconciler sent by god. . . . He combined

---

86. Ernst Käsemann, "Erwägungen zum Stichwort 'Versöhnungslehre im Neuen Testament,'" in *Zeit und Geschichte*, FS Bultmann (Tübingen: Mohr, 1964), 47–59.

in one what had been brought from everywhere. As in one loving cup he mingled lives, customs, marriages, and ways of life. He decreed that all should consider the entire inhabited world [*oikouménē*] their native city, his camp their acropolis and garrison, all good people their kinsfolk, and the wicked aliens."

Plutarch presents this reconciliation as the fulfillment of Zeno's utopian state (329 B), saying that this founder of the Stoic school had described "in the manner of a dream or shadow" how people should live without being separated according to the legal customs of their various cities and nations. They should instead regard all humanity as their compatriots. Zeno adds that "there is a common life and a single world, like a flock sharing a single pasture and feeding on a common pasture" (a play on *nómos*, which means both "law" and "pasture"). The contrast developed in 330 D is especially important as the model and counterpart for Pauline and pre-Pauline Christology:

> "[Alexander] did not fall on Asia like a robber; neither was he minded to dismember and exploit it like plunder [*hosper harpagma*] or booty.... Instead, he wanted all those dwelling upon the earth to obey a single purpose and a single state; he wanted to reveal that all humans constituted one people, and in like manner he shaped himself [*eschēmatízen*]."

Plutarch looks upon Alexander as having been sent to earth by the deity (*ho deūro katapémpsas tḗn Alexándrou psychḗn*). Still this very deity called him away before he had achieved his goal, that "a single law should govern all people, who should look up to a single justice [*hèn díkaion*] as to a single source of light." It was clear not only to Plutarch's readers but to all citizens of the Roman Empire that, ever since Augustus, the Caesars had taken over this role of Alexander the Great and brought to fruition what he had been unable to accomplish. The ubiquitous temples of Augustus give this notion visible expression, as the temple at Ancyra illustrates. Their outer walls recounted the *Acts of Augustus (Res Gestae)* in Greek translation, thereby making them accessible to the majority of the population of the Empire. The *Acts of Augustus* and the corresponding demonstrations of "saving" power became the gospel of the Caesar religion.

Gnostic influence certainly accounts for why Paul chose rebellion against God as the primary focus of reconciliation: men and women have become the enemies of God. Their enmity and rebellion is erased by the Christ event. But humanity is viewed as a whole not only in its negative aspect, rebellion, but also in its positive aspect, reconciliation. The pre-Christian Gnostic hymn in Col. 1:15-20[87] extols wisdom as mediator of creation, revealer, and savior. The world of death is powerless against her. Since wisdom governs creation and bestows unity on the world, she does not admit alienation or fragmentation. She causes the fullness of the new world to dwell within her and effects cosmic reconciliation and peace.[88] Here, too, there is an implicit critique of all forms of power. If even the cosmic powers engender alienation, fragmentation, chaos, and death when they are not subject to wisdom, so all the more must earthly powers—especially

87. The best study of this hymn is still that of Ernst Käsemann, "Eine urchristliche Taufliturgie," in *Festschrift Rudolf Bultmann*, ed. Ernst Wolf (Stuttgart: Kohlhammer, 1949), 133–48. The objections of scholars such as Lohse (Eduard Lohse, *A Commentary on the Epistles to the Colossians and Philemon* [Philadelphia: Fortress Press, 1971], 4) to the claim that the hymn is pre-Christian are not convincing. If the hymn is Christian, the absence of any reference to the historical existence of Jesus is astonishing. That it is not explained by Lohse and other critics of Käsemann is all the more astonishing, because even Lohse considers the references to the crucifixion (and the church) to be clearly extraneous and secondary additions. Wisdom influence, which even Lohse accepts, accounts for the biblical allusions. I have shown (in my "Der vorpaulinische Hymnus," in *Zeit und Geschichte*, 262–93, that the hymn in Philippians is also based on a pre-Christian hymn celebrating wisdom as revealer and savior.

88. The relationship between the primal human being and the savior can be described less abstractly than in the Colossians hymn, as one can see in both the Philippians hymn and Eph. 2:11-22. See also Brandenburger, *Adam und Christus*, 77–81.

when they imagine that they possess wisdom and engender order and blessing.[89]

The religion of Alexander and subsequently the Caesar religion avoided treating the death of their chief figures as a central event. They certainly did not treat it as salvific, not even in the case of Julius Caesar. To have done so would have robbed the active life of Alexander the Great and the Caesars who imitated him of its liberating and reconciling impact. Death would also have lost its function as the platform for ascension to the heavens; it would no longer have been secondary to sovereign triumph. Nevertheless, the motif of a vicarious death "for others" has its roots in Greek thought.[90] It plays an important role in Hellenism, not least through the influence of Greek tragedy, particularly the dramas of the Hellenistic world's most popular playwright Euripides. From this source, the concept that one person's suffering and death could efficaciously liberate many or all—the concept of heroic engagement and sacrifice—became a staple of education. The process was helped along by the use of this motif in philosophy.[91] Dating from the first century at the latest, 4 Maccabees

89. On the relationship between political establishment and the ideas of revelation and salvation typical of Gnostic wisdom, see Georgi, "Wesen der Weisheit," 77–81.

90. See Sam K. Williams, *Jesus' Death as Saving Event: The Background and Origin of a Concept*, Harvard Dissertations in Religion (Missoula: Scholars Press, 1975). On pp. 59–135, Williams shows that the commonly accepted theory tracing the motif of vicarious salvific suffering and death back to the Old Testament and Judaism is not convincing. On pp. 137–63, he discusses certain Hellenistic and Roman prototypes, citing popular examples on pp. 144-46. In n. 44 on p. 160, he cites the example of the legendary king Codros from the speech of the Hellenistic rhetor Lycurgus against Leocrates (84-88). Lycurgus seeks to show that "kings preferred to die for [*hypér*] the *sōtería* [salvation] of their subjects and to surrender their own lives instead of the common *sōtería*" (88). In *Symposium* 179 B, Plato states the general proposition that "only those who love are willing to die for others [*hyperapothnéskein*]," men as well as women. This passage is cited by Hans Windisch, *Der zweite Korintherbrief*, Kritisch-exegetisher Kommentar, 6, 9th ed. (Gottingen: Vandenhoeck & Ruprecht, 1924), 182. Livy lists examples of heroic sacrifice from the Roman past; we will not discuss the question of whether they really represent Roman tradition or reflect Hellenistic and Augustan influence. They clearly play into the hands of the theology and propaganda supporting the religion of the Caesars.

91. On the notion of the vicariously suffering philosopher, see Williams, *Back-*

shows that in the Hellenistic Jewish synagogue—probably influenced by Hellenistic missionary theology—the Jewish theology of martyrdom also had borrowed from paganism the idea of the vicarious suffering and death of male and female heroes.[92]

The notion that self-sacrifice for the good of others was the special province of sovereigns and other leaders and helped maintain society was still very much alive in the New Testament period. It was alive not least in philosophical circles, as well as in the Roman sagas restored in the Augustan and post-Augustan period.[93] In the religion and theology of Caesarism, however, the trend was to situate this perrogative (and duty) below the level of the sovereign.[94] In the first century

---

ground, pp. 138–44. With respect to Paul's controversy with his heroically minded opponents and the resulting debate over the *diákonos* (minister) concept, it is interesting that Epictetus (*Diss.* 3. 24.64–65) describes Diogenes as having demonstrated that he was a person sent by God (*diákonos Diós/theoū*) "by loving everyone and happily accepting all kinds of physical suffering and torment for the common good [*hypér toū koinoū*] of all."

92. Williams does not give sufficient weight to 4 Maccabees as reflecting synagogue preaching influenced by Hellenistic missionary theology.

93. See the examples of Codros and Diogenes in nn. 90, 91 above. The latter (though the motif of death is not present) extends the benefits of the philosopher's conduct to the whole human race. Livy (*Ab urbe condita* 8.6.8–16; 9.4–10.10) describes the sacrificial death of the consul Publius Decimus Mus in the battle against the Latins: on the basis of certain prodigies, he threw himself sacrificially upon the foe ("for the sake of legions"; "for the army"), thus bringing about the defeat of the enemy troops. Livy also claims (10.11–11.1) that this conduct was based on an ancient custom. Windisch (*Der zweite Korintherbrief*, 182) cites the example of Otho, who is quoted by Dio Cassius (*Hist.* 63.13) as saying prior to committing suicide: "It is better and more just that one should die for [*hypér*] all than many for one," and "All should learn from this deed that you [Otho's friends and soldiers] chose as *princeps* a man who did not sacrifice you for [*hypér*] his own sake but himself for you."

94. A typical example is *Aen.* 5.814–16 (likewise cited by Windisch, *Der zweite Korintherbrief*, 182), where Virgil has Neptune say to Venus: "He [Aeneas] will certainly reach the harbor of Avernus. There will be only one man [the helmsman Palihurus] for you to seek, because he is lost in the whirlpool. One head will be sacrificed for many."

political leaders no longer sacrificed themselves—only their subordinates, who were not as close to the divine.[95]

Paul has other ideas. In 2 Cor. 5:14-21, he borrows and amplifies the motif of love and solidarity implicit in the notion of vicarious death. Not only Jesus (v. 14) but also God (vv. 18, 19, 21) express solidarity with all in death. This death is not simply a transitional stage, in the sense of "per aspera ad astra," but a fundamental fact that henceforth is integral to human existence. To express this situation, Paul borrows motifs from the theology of the mysteries, particularly the integrating power of the death of the deity worshiped in the mysteries.[96] Paul both abbreviates and enlarges this relationship, thereby radicalizing the assertion of solidarity. On the one hand, he eliminates here the mystery rite that causes this integration (the rite of initiation, e.g., baptism); on the other, he extends to the whole human race the communal solidarity established within the mysteries.[97] The purpose clause in v. 15 refers to all humanity: all those who live are to live no longer for themselves but for him who died and was raised for them.

Like many of the parallel passages that discuss the sacrifice of a single person for many or all, 2 Corinthians 5 establishes a legal principle fundamental to the community in question—here the whole human race. In this case, as in many of the examples from Greek tragedy, this principle is in conflict with common practice and the norms that purportedly govern reality. Paul states this principle in v. 14, which speaks of the "love of Christ." It controls "us"; it constrains Paul, his colleagues, the faithful, indeed all humanity,[98] to conclude

95. The pretender to the principate Otho (see n. 93 above), who would seem to be an exception, is in fact only making a noble gesture of self-renunciation.

96. See, e.g., the significance of the death and burial of Osiris and Dionysus as described by Plutarch *De Iside et Osiride* 316E, 364F, 365A; cf. J. Gwyn Griffiths, *De Iside et Osiride* (Cambridge, Eng.: University of Wales Press, 1970), 71–73, 390ff.

97. There is no trace of any limitation to the faithful, as some exegetes continue to claim.

98. In 2 Cor. 2:14—7:4, Paul uses "we" very imprecisely, especially in chap. 5. Its range is greatest in 5:18-19, where "we" refers to all humankind in v. 18 but to

that life can be lived only for Jesus, who established his solidarity with all humankind. This legal principle is the new basis of human society. It is an obligation that "superiors," whether apostles or other leaders, cannot evade. It is true precisely because Jesus (and therefore, in Paul's view, God) has established and enjoined this fundamental principle of solidarity through personal sacrifice.

The allusions to the political propaganda of reconciliation that follow show that Paul is in critical antithesis to the Hellenistic society based on success, which claims to pursue equality. Everywhere, and above all in the Caesar religion, its ever-growing core, this society singles out the individual set apart by success—allegedly for the benefit, but in fact at the expense of the whole. Paul, however, asserts that since Jesus, humankind is not intrinsically controlled by competition and success, superiority and inferiority, superordination and subordination. Rather, humanity is controlled by the mutual solidarity of a life born out of a common death. From 2 Cor. 4:7-16, one knows that for Paul, this relationship with Jesus requires humans to take their own mortality with the utmost seriousness. This is underlined by the chapters of the so-called sorrowful letter in 2 Cor. 10–13. Only in dying with Jesus, in acceptance and acknowledgment of one's own frailty, in recognition of Jesus' indiscriminate solidarity with all and his renunciation of his own legal rights (5:21), only in such a way does authority make itself known, and all share in this authority. It is in this solidarity—not in success or power or fame—that righteousness and justice are to be found.

---

those who preach the gospel in v. 19. This lack of precision is pervasive and represents a deliberate ambivalence. Paul is concerned with the transparency of those who preach the gospel, open to the community and to the world, and he expects this openness also in return.

Philippians: A Disguised Affront

A short time after writing the letters containing the fragments in 2 Cor. 2:14—7:4 and 10–13, Paul was arrested at Ephesus and cast into a Roman prison.[99] In sharp contrast to Corinthians and Romans, Paul's correspondence with the Philippians during this imprisonment does not contain such unambiguous political and social allusions. But this very observation demonstrates the political nature of Pauline theology in general. Because he is in the hands of the Romans and therefore in immediate political danger, he has to be careful and change his tone. It is also characteristic, however, that he does not completely suppress the political and societal dimension in these letters written during his imprisonment, but rather disguises it. This is particularly evident in the fragments of the so-called joyful letter, Phil. 1:1—3:1 and 4:4-7. The last four verses appear to take a spiritualizing tack; but the repeated reference to Jesus as Lord brings to mind the hymn in 2:6-11, inculcating its significance for the whole.[100]

> [5]Have this mind among yourselves, which is yours in Christ Jesus, [6]who, though he was in the form of God, did not count equality with God a thing to be grasped, [7]but emptied himself, taking the form of a servant, being born in human likeness. [8]And being found in human form he humbled himself and became obedient unto death, even death on a cross. [9]Therefore God has highly exalted him and bestowed on him the name which is above every name, [10]that at the name of Jesus every knee should bow, in heaven and on earth

99. This imprisonment is discussed by Georgi, *Remembering the Poor.* For Paul's correspondence with the Philippians see ibid.

100. This connection with the hymn and its interpretation is even clearer if the reading of p[46] (*en kyríō Iēsoū,* "in the Lord Jesus") is correct. This variant has considerable validity: it appears to be the more difficult reading, and it is attested by a very early manuscript.

and under the earth, [11]and every tongue confess that
Jesus Christ is Lord, to the glory of God the Father.

The "Lord" of 2:6-11 has created a realm of peace in
which people can live secure (4:7) and in which all may
demonstrate royal forbearance (4:5).[101]

At first glance, the verses introducing the hymn in Phil.
2:6-11 appear also to reduce it to a spiritualized piece of
moralizing. They seem to take the edge off a text that defies
not just the world but all of its powers.

> [1]So if there is any encouragement in Christ, any
> incentive of love, any participation in the Spirit, any
> affection and sympathy, [2]complete my joy by being of
> the same mind, having the same love, being in full accord
> and of one mind. [3]Do nothing from selfishness or con-
> ceit, but in humility count others better than yourselves.
> [4]Let each of you look not only to his own interests, but
> also to the interests of others.

A superficial reading of 2:1-4 virtually embalms the words
that follow. But if one notes the bridge that joins the twin
phrases "in Christ" in vv. 1 and 5, then what is at issue in the
introductory exhortation is the realm of jurisdiction established by the Christ of the hymn and the very dynamics of his
rulership. Also at stake are the consequences of the act which,
with heavenly approval, has truly made Jesus the first among
equals: his obedience, his willingness to be subject to the
limits of the human condition. For Paul (the Roman citizen)
as well as for the citizens of Philippi (a military colony of
Rome) the description of Jesus' exaltation and entrance into
heaven must have suggested the events surrounding the de-
crease of a *princeps* and his heavenly assumption and apotheosis by resolution of the Roman senate, ratified in heaven.

101. Such "appropriateness" in the sense of "forbearance" or "gentleness" was
viewed especially by Hellenistic Judaism as a virtue of princes or princely people;
see Herbert Preisker, "epiekeia" in *TDNT*, 2:585–86.

By using a variety of paradoxes not only in its first but also in its second section, even the original, pre-Pauline hymn had turned the analogy into a critical antithesis. On the one hand, the name of the biblical God, to which all powers are subject, is bestowed upon Jesus; on the other, the simple name of Jesus is introduced into heaven and made the object for the oath of loyalty administered by all the powers.

Paul makes it absolutely impossible to misunderstand the movement of the hymn as suggesting a "per aspera ad astra" approach which would allow the exalted Lord to escape the limitations of human existence like the Caesars did. Paul, the Roman citizen, introduces into the text an affront that would be transparent to anyone familiar with Roman ways. The very death that makes Jesus the first among equals and equal to the biblical God is suffered neither in battle nor on a sickbed, but on the Roman cross. Such a death should have rendered his very memory accursed: a true *damnatio memoriae.* But more than his memory lives on: he himself does. This affront at the same time disguises what is for Paul the critical sting of the text, its tangible political and social threat: no Roman censor would think it necessary to fear a crucified pretender and a group of his followers. He would rank such a notion as an absurdity. In this fashion, nevertheless, Paul launches a critical infiltration of the reigning political and social principles.

That Paul is concerned in Phil. 2:6-11 with more than privatized relationships between individuals, not to mention a simply sectarian mentality, is shown by the following verse. Here, among other things, he calls upon his readers to "shine as lights in the world," "in the midst of a crooked and perverse generation" (v. 15). There are parallels in the political symbolism of antiquity for describing human beings as "semaphors" and "stars."

Beginning with Plato's simile of the cave in the seventh book of the *Republic*, Hellenism associated civic education and statemanship with light in a variety of ways. The Stoics incorporated light into their view of the cosmos as the authentic city state, wonderfully ordered. Chrysippus added the notion that the heavenly bodies are the citizens and magistrates of this *polis*.[102] This image is more than a metaphor: it is meant as a paradigm and admonition. In Cicero's *Somnium Scipionis*, the climax of his equivalent to Plato's *Republic*, Scipio is admonished to show the republic "the light of his soul." Elsewhere, in a similar vein, Cicero speaks of eminent individuals as "luminaries of the state." The "soul" (*animus*) comes down from the heavenly fire of the stars. It is trapped in an earthly body, which it can escape to return to the stars only by serving the body politic. This leads to the admonition[103] to follow these promptings of the heavenly fire within oneself: "Train (the soul) in the best of things." The best tasks are those that serve the good [*salus* = *sōtēría* = Phil. 2:12] of the fatherland. An *animus* thus prompted and exercised will fly more quickly back to this its seat and home. And it will accomplish this even more quickly if, while it is still in the body, it shines forth and observes what lies beyond, thus abstracting itself from the body as fully as possible." By way of contrast, Cicero describes the *animi* of those "who surrender to the passions of the body, virtually becoming their slaves; driven by their appetites, they obey these passions and violate the rights of gods and mortals."

Of course I am not suggesting that Paul had read Plato or Cicero. But the political ethics promoted by Cicero were not his own invention; in large measure, they were a common heritage. This heritage was shared above all by the following age and its civic education, on which the view espoused by Cicero had enormous posthumous influence, despite the changes of party politics. Cicero contributed substantially to the later development of the ideal of the *princeps*.[104]

Philo demonstrates that this blend of Stoicism and mysticism likewise had influenced the Hellenistic synagogue and

102. Plutarch *De communibus notitiis* 1076; cf. also Philo's proselytizing *De specialibus legibus* 1.13–14.

103. Cicero *Respublica* 6.26, 28–29.

104. See Cicero *Phil.* 8.22; 14.17; *Manil.* 41; *Dom.* 66; *Sest.* 98; *Fin.* 4.61; *Div.* 2.11; *Acad. pr.* 2.5–6; *Tusc.* 4.5; *Off.* 2.77; 3.74; *Resp.* 1.65.

its political ethics, although there the mystical component was not as consistently dualistic as in Cicero or Seneca. In the "Gnostic" Philo, however, this dualism was even more pronounced—to the point of virtual schizophrenia.[105]

Jewish apocalyptic has no bearing on Phil. 2:15, which speaks not of future reward[106] but of present reality. For the ideological locus of the Philippians text, it is also important to note the role played by light symbolism (and especially the stars) in the Caesar religion. A famous example is the denarius, now in the British Museum, bearing an image of the comet that appeared during the games sponsored by Octavian to celebrate Caesar's victory at Thapsus. It bears the inscription DIVUS IULIUS ("the divine Julius").

In short, in Phil. 2:15 Paul suggests to his Philippian readers that he would like to see them all as competitors of the statesmen who govern the present world. The latter rule as an elite, literally as "stars," over chaos, the chaos of a "crooked and perverse generation." The followers of Jesus on the other hand—none excluded, none preeminent—represent the authentic ruler of the human race, Jesus the truly human person. In so doing, they avail themselves of the only appropriate possibility for exercising political responsibility.

In the other fragment of the Philippian correspondence (3:2—4:3; 4:8-9) Paul uses the highly political term *políteuma* (3:20). The Cicero passage cited above makes the generally accepted "apolitical" interpretation of this word suspect. This is especially so if one makes allowance for the change in tactics forced upon the prisoner,[107] who resorts to a "spiritualizing" cover. Paul says: "Our *políteuma* is in heaven, whence we await the Lord Jesus Christ as savior." Several elements in this fragment recall Cicero: separation from those whose god is their belly and whose minds are set on "earthly things" (vv. 18-19); speculatively dualistic justification for a

105. See pp. 12–16 above.
106. See the passages cited by Hans Conzelmann, "phōs," in *TDNT*, 9:302–49, n. 285.
107. See p. 72 above.

discipline of work (3:7-14) (introduced as a model in vv. 15-17 and interpreted as an expression of an "upward call" (v. 14)—without, however, any hint of astral mysticism); an appeal for discipline and responsible action within the community (4:1-4); and a massively secular call for eclectic imagination in questions of ethical values (4:8-9). All of the foregoing fits the context of the political ethics cultivated at Rome at least as early as Cicero (and not unfamiliar to Seneca): a mixture of dualistic mysticism and Stoic ideas.

Roman political ethics also had an eschatological dimension, and the notion of a radical decision reminiscent of conversion was not ruled out. There were thus links between Paul and this political ethics, something like a common ground for dialogue. But on this foundation Paul constructs a critical alternative. It does not consist in renouncing the world. It has been shown above that worldly renunciation—if the concept is applicable at all in this dialogue—was the choice of the Roman political elite.

Paul's proposition takes issue with this political ethics in several essential features. Paul finds a place for human weakness and disgrace (3:4b-14); he democratizes his model by multiplication (3:15-17); he insists on discernment, understanding, and respectful inclusiveness. In this regard, Phil. 4:1-3 and 4:8-9 are especially important, following as they do the relatively stereotyped expression of anger in 3:18-19. A further critical difference is implied in 3:21. Here, the future resurrection envisioned (circumscribed as a transformation of the lowly body into a glorious body) concludes with the words "by the power which enables him even to subject the universe to himself."[108] Behind the awaited transformation stands the same power which, according to the hymn in Philippians, forced and still forces all other powers to acknowledge Jesus. Renunciation of ascendancy is the secret of as-

---

108. The nonreflexive reading *autō̃*, echoing 1 Cor. 15:28, makes a "theological" interpretation of the passage easier, thus reducing the challenge of the Pauline text, whereas in fact Phil. 3:21 picks up again the emphatic christological conclusion to the hymn in Phil. 2:6-11, i.e., the centerpiece of the previous epistolary fragment.

cendancy. Jesus' obedience is the mystery of his "glory" and establishes his rule. It puts an end to the hegemonic claims of all alienating and murderous power and violence together with their law.[109]

---

109. The position under attack in Phil. 3:2—4:3 and 4:8-9 is also oriented toward the law, as the introduction (3:1-6) makes clear. See Georgi, *Remembering the Poor.*

4

GOD TURNED UPSIDE DOWN

IN NONE OF PAUL'S EXTANT LETTERS does he take issue
with a form of Judaism resembling that which one encounters
in the rabinic literature based on the tradition of the Pharisees.
Even when—as in Galatians and 2 Corinthians—there is good
reason to associate Paul's opponents with Palestine, the Judaism they represent is fundamentally that of the diaspora.
Neither is the Judaism from which Paul springs and with which
he grapples a ghetto phenomenon. On the contrary: it is in
active dialogue and exchange with the pagan world of Hellenism. Whatever the local varieties of diaspora Judaism may
have been, they all consciously reflect the universal problems
of their contemporary culture and society. They do not do so,
however, at the expense of their Judaism, which they understand as the truest representation of what they held to be the
core of Hellenistic civilization.

The Jewish problems that Paul discusses, including what
one might call segregationist aloofness and even bodily mutilation in honor of the deity, were not that particularistic. They
reflected socio-religious problems of the whole Hellenistic
world as well. The Jewish sense of being a chosen people

has its counterpart among the Greeks and is even more pro-nounced among the Romans. But those who are chosen do not consider their election a peripheral phenomenon. Rather, it places them in the very center of the world, and they un-derstand themselves as authentic representatives of univer-sal—i.e., Hellenistic—civilization.[1] Religiously motivated sur-gical manipulation, especially as a sign of belonging to a particular group or elite, was not limited to the Jews. It was known in the Eastern Mediteranean and in Africa (Egypt and Ethiopia) as well. It is discussed as a borderline of what a religion can demand—even in a pluralistic society. Thus Paul's controversies with the Jews are at the same time representative critical approaches to universal problems confronting Hel-lenism in the first century.

This is absolutely clear in Romans. Here in particular Paul sets his sights on the branch of the Jewish wisdom movement that is in my opinion the most "modern," or comes closest to Protestantism: Jewish missionary theology. This theology was a liberal and universalist movement, the essence and driving force of Judaism as a world religion. It was the most successful missionary movement prior to Christianity.[2]

1. For a discussion of diaspora Judaism, see Dieter Georgi, *The Opponents of Paul in Second Corinthians* (Philadelphia: Fortress Press, 1986), passim, and esp. the epilogue. For examples of bodily mutilation, which in most instances is religiously motivated, even when this is not stated explicitly, see Diodorus Siculus 1.28, 55; 3.32; Strabo 3.5, 9; 16.2, 34, 37; 16.4, 5, 9, 10, 17; 17.2, 5; Josephus *Apion* 1. 169–71, 214; 2.141–42; idem, *Antiquities* 1. 214.

2. The similarity of Rom. 1:18-32 to Jewish apologetics, i.e., missionary theology, has often been noted. See the commentaries of Ernst Käsemann, *Commentary on Romans* (Grand Rapids, Mich.: Eerdmans, 1980); and Ulrich Wilckens, *Der Brief an die Römer*, Kommentar zum Neuen Testament 6 (Cologne: Benziger; Neukirchen: Neukirchener Verlag, 1978–82); and esp. Günther Bornkamm, "Die Offenbarung des Zornes Gottes (Röm. 1–3)," in *Das Ende des Gesetzes: Paulusstudien*, in his *Ges-ammelte Aufsätze*, 1, 2d ed., Beiträge zur Evangelischen Theologie 16 (Munich: Chr. Kaiser, 1958), 9–33. Paul's description of the abominations of the Gentiles (1:21-32) and his mention at the outset (1:19-20) of the knowledge available to them from the works of God sound like a paraphrase of missionary preaching in the Jewish syn-agogue, save that Paul—influenced by apocalypticism and Gnosticism—comes to an entirely negative conclusion, rejecting any missionary point of connection. Citing several passages in Romans 2:1—3:20, Bornkamm also notes certain relations with

Romans: Jewish Missionary Theology and Roman Political Theology

Paul's dispute with "liberal" Judaism is concerned fundamentally with the contemporary strategy of social consensus.
Jewish missionary theology was a highly developed expression of this strategy, which in its pagan manifestation in Rome
culminated in the Caesar religion. Paul focused on Judaism
not simply because the Jesus movement was of Jewish origin,
and therefore found its first critical dialogue in this milieu,
but also because he could use it to disguise his political
program. Debate with Judaism was the code for a more far-
ranging conflict that brought Paul into mortal danger. He later
fell victim to this danger in the very city of Rome.

Strategies of social consensus—especially those of the
first century—tend to concentrate on developing a legal system that expresses the institutional form of the desired social
utopia. This concentration on law was also characteristic of
Jewish missionary theology during the first century. But it is
not only the centrality of tradition that speaks here. It is also
Judaism's imaginative preoccupation with the law, which was
the essential contribution it had to offer the present and the
future. The Jewish mission did not address only Jewish believers and their institutions in the spirit of apologetics or
reform. It also addressed the Hellenistic world and each of
its institutions, including the Roman state. What the Jewish

---

discussions between Hellenistic Jews and Hellenistic pagans, with which Paul was
probably familiar through his education in the Jewish wisdom tradition and
his exposure to Hellenistic Jewish diaspora preaching. That Paul has this missionary propaganda in view in Romans and concentrates on it becomes finally clear in
2:17-29.

The forms and concepts of Jewish worship in the diaspora and of the Jewish
wisdom tradition have put their stamp on the entire Pauline corpus. We have already
encountered Jewish missionary theology in particular as a critical background in
Galatians (see pp. 33–52 above). Above all, however, Paul's opponents in 2 Corinthians represent an adaptation of this theology to Jesus (see pp. 61–71 above).

missionary theologians had to offer was a "liberal" law. For the Jewish missionaries as well as for their partners in dialogue—Jews and Gentiles alike—the strategy of consensus which the Jewish law offered was not only theoretical but also practical, not only religious but also social. The extent of this concern with the law is illustrated, for example, by Philo's discussion of the Mosaic law and by Josephus' treatment of the same theme. It is also illustrated by the way both individuals dealt with the Roman bureaucracy.

It is this praxis, as well as an alternative one, that are the subject of Romans. It would be wrong to suppose that only the alternative praxis which Paul discusses with the community in Rome had something to do with eschatology. During the first century, the social praxis of both paganism and Judaism, above all "apologetic," "liberal" Judaism, was shaped by eschatology. It aimed to realize a concrete utopian design.[3]

Romans, Paul's last extant letter, summarizes his varied experiments, both practical and theoretical, in a single grand outline. It is this outline that he sends to the congregation of Jesus' followers in Rome, both as introduction and as groundwork for his prospective conversation with them.[4] In the first chapter Paul suggests (and states explicitly in 15:20) that visiting Rome would actually run counter to his own principles because a congregation of Jesus' followers already existed there. By insisting on this visit, a "temporary sojourn," Paul violated these principles. In doing so he indicates that this city has a special significance, which makes him not want to bypass it. What could this significance be other than its position as world capital?

3. On the eschatology of Jewish missionary theology, see Georgi, *Opponents*, 148–51. In the epilogue (p. 376 n. 334), I also discuss the eschatology of contemporary Roman political theology; see Dieter Georgi, "Who Is the True Prophet," in *Christians Among Jews and Gentiles,* ed. George W. Nickelsburg, George W. MacRae (Philadelphia: Fortress Press, 1986), 100–26.

4. On Romans as a summary of Paul's earlier theological sketches, see Günther Bornkamm, "Der Römerbrief als Testament des Paulus," in *Geschichte und Glaube, Teil 2,* in his *Gesammelte Aufsätze*, 4, Beiträge zur Evangelischen Theologie 53 (Munich: Chr. Kaiser, 1971), 1201–39.

Furthermore, every page of the letter contains indications that Paul has very concrete and critical objections to the dominant political theology of the Roman Empire under the principate. By using such loaded terms as *euangélion, pístis, dikaiosýnē,* and *eirēnē* as central concepts in Romans, he evokes their associations to Roman political theology. Monuments of this theology were familiar to his contemporaries throughout the Empire, both east and west. And everyone carried the flyers of this ideology about in the form of Roman coins.

All attempts to derive the Pauline use of *euangélion* (gospel) from the Septuagint have failed. The noun does not appear there with the Pauline double meaning, which denotes both the act and the content of proclamation. Nevertheless, in extrabiblical Greek usage the term possesses a dynamic meaning that also embraces content and action. The dynamic tendency finds expression above all in the predominance of the plural. The closest parallel (albeit in the plural) to the Pauline usage of *euangélion* occurs in an inscription from Priene.[5] At the suggestion of the Roman proconsul, this city decided to shift the beginning of the new year, and thus the installation of all city officials, to September 23, the birthday of Augustus. The shift was made on the grounds that this day had given a new aspect, as it were, to the universe and marked a new beginning for all things.

This savior (*soter*) had above all brought the world peace. But among his other benefactions he also had created an order of fairness in all matters. The variety in this salutary experience is reflected in the spreading of the message of universal salvation like a grass-fire (whence the plural). The Caesar-religion is based primarily on these tidings.

The word *pistis* has been encountered already in Galatians 2 and 3. One can see there that the translation "faith" does not exhaust its meaning. "Faithfulness" or "loyalty,"

---

5. Wilhelm Dittenberger, *Sylloge Inscriptionum Graecarum*, 3d ed. (Leipzig: Hirzel, 1915-24), 458.

which includes the notion of "trust," comes nearer to the Pauline usage of the term. This more objective sense of the Greek word from Gal. 3:23-25 is maintained in Romans. Rom. 3:3 uses it to speak expressly of God's "faithfulness" or "reliability." I want also to point to the Greek translation of the *Acts of Augustus*. This fundamental gospel of the Caesar-religion speaks of *pístis*. There, in the context of chapters 31-33, which describe universal friendship with foreign powers and rulers, one finds the summary statement that under the principate of Augustus many previously unbefriended peoples "discovered the *pistis* of the Roman people." Beginning in the time of Augustus, *fides*, the Latin synonym of *pistis*, was reassessed and assumed weightier dimensions.

The Caesar represented the *fides* of Rome in the sense of loyalty, faithfulness to treaty obligations, uprightness, truthfulness, honesty, confidence, and conviction—all, as it were, a Roman monopoly. The ancient cult of the goddess Fides was revived under Augustus. It is significant too, in the period of the principate, that the word appears frequently on coins.[6] What was said above[7] about the objective character of *pístis* and its Gnostic background takes on an especially critical relevance in the light of this objectivized religious concept in contemporary Roman religion.

The *Acts of Augustus* also speak of *dikaiosýnē* (chap. 34) as one of the four attributes demonstrated by Augustus and recognized by law. By decree of the senate and the popular assembly, the attributes were inscribed upon golden plates and presented to the *princeps*.[8] It is also noteworthy that Ovid, describing the dedication of a temple to Justitia,[9] identifies the *princeps* with Justitia.[10] On the whole, however, the Pauline

6. See also Werner Eisenhut, "Fides," in *Der kleine Pauly* (Stuttgart: Druckenmüller, 1964), 2:545–46; and H. Le Bonniec, "Fides," in *Lexikon der Alten Welt* (Zurich: Artemis, 1965), 969.

7. See p. 36, n.10; p. 43.

8. *Corpus Inscriptionum Latinarum*, 9:5811.

9. Ovid *Ex Ponto* 3.6.23–29.

10. "Iampridem posuit mentis in aede suae" ("long ago already he has enshrined her—justice—in the temple of his mind").

term *dikaiosýnē* is derived more from the Jewish Bible. As I already argued in discussing Galatians 2,[11] it denotes first and foremost the solidarity of God with mortals.

The peace ideology of the Roman Empire had long been a force in Roman praxis and propaganda. It achieved world-wide recognition in consequence of the miraculous peace established by Augustus. The statistics of *eirēnē* in Paul suggest that he is looking for critical engagement with this ideology. In Romans, the theme of peace plays a more extensive role than anywhere else in Paul (or the remainder of the New Testament): the word *eirēnē* appears ten times, the expression "to have peace" once. There are also many words of related meaning: *dikaiosýnē, cháris, chára, oikodomé, zoé, elpis* ("solidarity, grace, joy, constructive activity, life, hope").

Almost all the Pauline letters proceed by interpreting in the body of the epistle the traditional formulas or phrases appearing either at the beginning or in the introduction. This is also true in Romans, where the formula is found in 1:3-4:[12]

> "...the gospel concerning [God's] Son, who was descended from David according to the flesh and designated Son of God in power according to the Spirit of holiness by his resurrection from the dead, Jesus Christ our Lord."

The exegete must explain why a text like this should be cited in a letter addressed to the seat of Roman power. The formula, which speaks of the origins and significance of the royal messiah Jesus, reflects the two-phase structure of the biblical law of kingship.[13] More is at stake here than spiritualized religious questions.

11. See p. 36 above.
12. See the detailed discussion of these verses in Käsemann, *Römer*, 8–11; and Wilckens, *Römer*, 1:56–61, 64–66.
13. The future king was first declared God's elect by prophetic designation and then, in a second step, adopted as God's son, i.e., enthroned as king. In the case of the kings of Judah, the oracle of the prophet Nathan assumed once and for all the function of prophetic designation. It was interpreted as applying to the entire dynasty—the phrase "from the seed of David" in Rom. 1:3-4.

In Romans, Paul introduces the figure he considers to be the true king into the kingship debate. The antagonist is not so much the royal messiah of Jewish missionary theology; this figure enters into the picture, but not in any pivotal role. The adversary is rather a different figure, a power that in fact considers itself politically and religiously central, a force that claims universal dominion in the political and social realm but bases this claim on a religion and a theology: the Roman Caesar. Here, in Romans, there is a critical counterpart to the central institution of the Roman Empire. This institution, after all, purported to hold the world together, and even for Jews represented a worldwide society. It was a power that in the first century was still looked upon as a savior throughout the world—not only by the upper-class elite but also by a broad cross-section of the lower classes.

Speaking out of the Jesus tradition of Hellenistic Judaism, Paul introduces the Nazarene as the true king in Rom. 1:3-4. But are not his qualifications and the circumstances of his accession rather dubious? By "normal" standards, there is something highly irregular here. Is an element of satire intended? A year before Paul wrote Romans,[14] a change of regime had taken place in Rome under most unusual circumstances. Following the violent death of Claudius, the senate decreed his *consecratio*—i.e., not only his life after death but also his assumption and apotheosis. Among other things, this event evoked the ridicule of Seneca in his satirical *Apocolocyn-thosis*, "The Pumpkinification of Claudius." Claudius' violent death brought Nero to the throne. But Jesus, too, came to power through a violent death—in this case his own—which was brought about by the Romans.

Paul's use of terminology drawn from the law of royal succession in Rom. 1:3-4 shows that he is making more than a religious claim. The following verse shows that something more is involved than nationalistic Jewish propaganda. Is Paul using the traditional formula in order to support an alternative

14. See Dieter Georgi, *Remembering the Poor* (Decatur: Abingdon, forthcoming).

theory concerning true rulership and the legitimate *princeps*? Is he offering an alternative to the social utopia of Caesarism, with its promise of universal reconciliation and peace as the prerequisite for undreamed of achievements resulting in unimagined prosperity? Roughly contemporary with Romans are the two fragmentary eclogues of the Einsiedeln Papyrus that celebrate the accession of the young Nero as the beginning of the golden age. Is it Paul's intention to measure King Jesus and his program by this yardstick?

The first step in Paul's exposition of the Christ formula is Rom. 1:5. Here he interprets apostolic preaching as a mission to the peoples.[15] In 1:14, Paul speaks of his obligation to both Greeks and barbarians, a typical formula in Hellenistic propaganda, especially political propaganda, for the unity of the human race. This mission is led by the brush-fire of the good news of Jesus.

If the terms chosen by Paul for his Roman readers have associations with the slogans of Caesar religion, then Paul's gospel must be understood as competing with the gospel of the Caesars. Paul's gospel enters into critical dialogue with the good news that universal peace has been achieved by the miracle of Actium. This was a prodigious miracle that brought respite and new life to a world tortured by a century of civil war. Even a devout Jew like Philo could celebrate this marvel, secured by the law and might of Rome.[16] The *sōtēría* represented by Caesar and his empire is challenged by the *sōtēría* brought about by Jesus. Like that of Caesar, the *sōtēría* of the God Jesus is worldwide (1:16).

15. By *éthnē*, Paul means all the nations, not simply the Gentiles. I have already pointed out (p. 61) that even the biblical prophets thought of themselves as prophets to the peoples of the world. Furthermore, when compared with the remaining letter, Rom. 1:5 does not suggest that Paul is using "we" simply to refer to himself. In 1:8-15 and 15:14-32, where he discusses his personal intentions with respect to Rome, he uses the first person singular. Paul stands to gain strong support for his trip to Rome if he can show that his sense of having a worldwide mission is not his own invention but that a mission to the nations is fundamental to the apostolate. Rome, the capital of the world, belongs to everyone; it is certainly justifiable and appropriate that the apostles, who are sent to the peoples of the world, should visit it.

16. See p. 15 above.

But here I have already come to Paul's next step in his interpretation of Jesus' kingship—his concentration on God's loyalty (*pístis*) as affirmed and expressed in God's solidarity (*dikaiosýnē*) with the human race. The good news of Jesus refuses to employ threats and the exercise of power and violence—even the law—as instruments of rulership. According to Paul, the *sōtēría* of the God Jesus has made loyalty a two-way street (*ek písteōs eis pístin* 1:16): it demonstrates and creates loyalty, but demands loyalty as well (1:16-17).

In 1:18—3:20, Paul shows why the active authority and salvation of Jesus, the king described in Rom. 1:3-4, cannot be based on the instrumentality of the law. Even more vigorously than in Galatians, Paul debates the widespread universalist understanding of the law,[17] which identifies God's law with the law that governs the world. He also debates the claim that acceptance of this law could bring about the unity of the human race, a unity envisioned not as uniformity but as pluralistic variety. The two outstanding representatives of this view of the law were Roman political theology and Jewish missionary theology. Roman political theology also harbored missionary ambitions, reflected in the double program of education and the expanding Caesar religion. When Paul takes a critical look at Jewish missionary theology in 1:18—3:20 (and elsewhere in Romans) his eye is also on the Caesar religion and the theology underpinning it.

It is therefore the "liberal" and "humane"—even "humanistic"—understanding of the law inherent in such religious options that Paul subjects to radical criticism in Rom. 1:8—3:20 (and elsewhere in the letter). Jewish missionary theology and Roman political theology speak of the deity as exercising sovereignty through the law, bestowing blessings, and establishing and preserving universal community. In Rom. 1:18—3:20, Paul insists that the law signifies and creates chaos, and that those who appeal to it are unmasked as transgressors. The orderly and upstanding citizens turn out to be

---

17. See pp. 6, 33–34 above.

rebels, perverting themselves and humanity. Instead of saving the world, they plunge it into ruin. There is no solidarity among those who are ruled by the law, neither with God nor among themselves. Those who think they are privileged because of their obedience to the law are not exempt from this catastrophe.[18] In 1:18—3:20, Paul does not speak of a doom to come but of a present reality that determines the fate of the entire human race.[19]

I have already pointed out[20] that the various universalistic conceptions of law in the first century operated with highly concrete ideas of an elite which embodies in tangible human form the pinnacle of God's law and God's sovereignty over this world. This embodiment appeared in the form of dominant groups and their traditions (above all Jews and Romans). It was also seen to be embodied in individuals specially

18. In order to understand Paul's discussion of the law, it is important to note in Rom. 2:1 that, although he is undoubtedly thinking primarily of the Jews, he does not say so explicitly, but expresses himself in general terms. Basically, he is talking about all allegiance to the obligations imposed by any law whatever. According to Paul, those who are "upright" and "respectable" are not entitled to dissociate themselves from the "lawbreakers." Both the upright and the lawbreakers are disastrously subject to the demands of the law. They are cut from the same cloth and, therefore, share a common fate.

19. This present reality which is under discussion in Rom. 1:18—3:20 has been brought out above all by Bornkamm in "Die Offenbarung des Zorn Gottes." He has also shown that Paul is not trying to describe a subject of common knowledge in this delineation of universal doom—certainly not a shared basis on which any individual might develop a knowledge of God. What is described depends on the revelation and judgment of God. On pp. 30–33, Bornkamm also shows that the revelation asserted in 1:18—3:20 cannot be understood apart from the revelation in Rom. 3:21-31, an important insight that also bears on Rom. 7:7-24. "When he uses the eschatological terms *orgé theoū* ["wrath of God"] and *apokalýptesthai* ["to reveal"] and connects 1:18 so closely with 1:17, this obviously means that only now, in the sign of the gospel, has the lost world been brought into the light of the *éschaton*. . . . The attention of the world can be called to signs showing that it is lost and thus to the trend its history has taken under the hand of God's judgment; but it needs to be told explicitly that its imprisonment in sin is so radical that the history of the world is already illuminated, so to speak, by the glare of the last judgment. This does not follow from the principles of what the world already knows, though in the Apostle's opinion, both Gentiles and Jews are perfectly able to understand it" (p. 31).

20. See pp. 12–16, 61–63 above.

associated with the deity, the *theîoi anthropoi*, the great personalities of the past and the present. Among these the Roman *princeps* naturally played an outstanding role, acknowledged (at least in the figure of Augustus) even by the Jew Philo.

Paul's opponents in 2 Corinthians were influenced by Jewish missionary theology and its kindred social ideas. In attacking these "great personalities" Paul attempted to show that their actions represented a conspiracy of the elite against society—or, to use the body metaphor of Roman political theology, a revolt of the head against the body. The sarcasm of Paul's critique in Rom. 2:1-29 is aimed at those who pass judgment, in particular the proselytizing Jews, whose criticism of the evils of paganism Paul has just paraphrased. But 2:1-29 is also meant paradigmatically. It is an exemplary attack on all who consider themselves above the "common" people—all who think they are morally superior and therefore qualified to govern the "mob." Those who claim to be superior, in reality, are nothing but engines of revolt. They seduce others to join the rebellion they embody. It is they who are the real conspirators, drawing humanity on to catastrophe.

What the Hellenistic world (especially its Jewish or Roman philosophical circles) concretely meant by the dominion of God (or the gods) which was exercised through the law is also discussed, albeit "retrospectively,"[21] in Rom. 7:7-24.

[7]What then shall we say? That the law is sin? By no means! Yet, if it had not been for the law, I should not have known sin. I should not have known what it

---

21. See Werner Georg Kümmel, *Römer 7 und die Bekehrung des Paulus* (Leipzig: Hinrichs, 1929); Rudolf Bultmann, "Romer 7 und die Anthropologie des Paulus," in *Imago Dei: Beiträge zur theologischen Anthropologie, Festschrift Gustav Krüger*, Heinrich Bornkamm, ed. (Giessen: Töpelmann, 1932), 53–62. These scholars have shown clearly that this section is not autobiographical; neither does it describe a "natural" human insight. The discussion is not in the least subjective. As Bultmann puts it (p. 53): "Here Paul describes the situation of all those who are subject to the law, as made visible to the eyes of those who have been set free from the law through Christ."

is to covet if the law had not said, "You shall not covet." [8]But sin, finding opportunity in the commandment, wrought in me all kinds of covetousness. Apart from the law sin lies dead. [9]I was once alive apart from the law, but when the commandment came, sin revived and I died; [10]the very commandment which promised life proved to be death to me. [11]For sin, finding opportunity in the commandment, deceived me and by it killed me. [12]So the law is holy, and the commandment is holy and just and good.

[13]Did that which is good, then, bring death to me? By no means! It was sin, working death in me through what is good, in order that sin might be shown to be sin, and through the commandment might become sinful beyond measure. [14]We know that the law is spiritual; but I am carnal, sold under sin. [15]I do no understand my own actions. For I do not do what I want, but I do the very thing I hate. [16]Now if I do what I do not want, I agree that the law is good. [17]So then it is no longer I that do it, but sin which dwells within me. [18]For I know that nothing good dwells within me, that is, in my flesh. I can will what is right, but I cannot do it. [19]For I do not do the good I want, but the evil I do not want is what I do. [20]Now if I do what I do not want, it is no longer I that do it, but sin which dwells within me.

[21]So I find it to be a law that when I want to do right, evil lies close at hand. [22]For I delight in the law of God, in my inmost self, [23]but I see in my members another law at war with the law of my mind and making me captive to the law of sin which dwells in my members. [24]Wretched man that I am! Who will deliver me from this body of death?

Here Paul returns to the theme expounded in 1:18—3:20—that the end of the law is chaos—and develops it further. As the introductory verses of chap. 7 show, Paul has in mind not only the Jewish law, or a particular religious law of any sort. He also is considering law in general, including the civil law regulating society—in particular, Roman law.[22] The will of the deity is seen to be also (and particularly) manifested in the law that governs society. Josiah Royce,[23] though not trained in technical exegesis, anticipated the insights of Kümmel and Bultmann by decades. He observed that Paul uses "law" in Romans 7 to denote not only the will of God but the will and consensus of society. It is the unfortunate nature of such a transcendent will—especially the collective will—that its demands generate and encourage consciousness of self.[24]

22. Käsemann says (*Romans*, 187): "*Nomos* here is simply the legal order . . . to which the citizens of the capital were subject and which would not be beyond their legal knowledge. They were not barbarians." Seen in the context of the chapters that precede and follow, the religiously neutral language of Romans 7 is remarkable. Only vv. 4 and 25 refer explicitly to Christ and God. Verse 22 may also refer to God, although the text *tō nómō toū noós* ("law of the mind") seems preferable, since the genitive *theoū* ("God") is certainly the easier reading theologically. However that may be, the *nómos* in question is synonymous with the *nómos toū noós mou* ("law of my mind") of v. 23. Some exegetes claim that the scribe of Codex Vaticanus was anticipating the latter phrase, but this explanation seems to me less likely. In either case, it is difficult to connect the *nómou toū noós mou* of v. 23 with the Torah from Sinai. Such an identification would require at least some measure of Philonic mediation. More likely the phrase refers to "good law" in general, of whatever provenance.

23. Josiah Royce discusses Romans 7 in Lecture 3 of his *The Problem of Christianity* (New York: Macmillan Co., 1913; reprint, Chicago: Henry Regnery, 1968), 1:107–59.

24. On this point, Royce is in agreement with Bultmann ("Römer 7," pp. 61–63): "Sin is thus the human desire to be in control, the assertion one's own claims, the desire to be like God." Both also agree that we are dealing here with "transsubjective processes," i.e., beyond individual choices and decisions. Royce, however, by using social categories and concentrating on social psychology rather than individual psychology, seems more in tune with the concreteness and dramatic force of Paul's argument than is Bultmann with his highly abstract discourse. As Ernst Fuchs has correctly noted (*Die Freiheit des Glaubens: Römer 5–8 ausgelegt*, Beiträge zur evangelischen Theologie 14 [Munich: Chr. Kaiser, 1949], 55–83), Paul's discussion has dimensions that are clearly mythological, although I cannot agree with Fuchs's reconstructions. Romans 7:7-24 describes an authentic tragedy. Here Paul comes closest to the tragic schema of Gnosticism, undoubtedly with full awareness of what he is doing. It is characteristic of Paul's way of dealing with Gnosticism, however, that he places 7:7-24 in its present context rather than earlier—replacing 1:18—3:20, for example, with which it has much in common, or even before 1:16. Paul can likewise speak of salvation for the wicked who do not know God, a concept unknown

The result is individualism, social differentiation, and division of labor.[25] Hence arise competition, greed, conflict, contentiousness, avarice, self-assertion, and disunity.[26]

This conflict in turn attacks the law itself (7:14-24). It splits apart *de facto* into two laws: the will of society and the will of the individual. Both are mutually dependent, and this interdependence conditions their fundamental conflict: inherent mutual hatred (v. 23). Even the conscience is drawn into this vicious circle. It is neither a neutral arbiter nor—as the discoverers of conscience (Philo, and other later Hellenistic and Roman philosophers) would have it—an ethical guide.[27] According to Royce's perceptive interpretation of Rom. 7:14-24, conscience arises from the chaos of the intersecting conflicts between society and individuals, between law and law (vv. 22-23). Individualism and collectivism are mutually dependent and create an impenetrable maze. The cooperation that the societal will promises to bring about generates neither affection nor understanding. Rather, it generates only competition among individuals who are fundamentally at odds. The flesh is not just an element of each individual, a moral evil. It is sinful activity *par excellence*— the competitive struggle and divisive conflict dictated by the will of society. It is therefore a destructive power; it is enslavement. The societal process brings forth both conscious and conscientious sinners.

In Rom. 3:21-26, as in his earlier letters, Paul counters this fateful rule of law with the death of Jesus.

---

to Gnosticism. By thus eliminating even the last traces of elitism, Paul intensifies the Gnostic protest.

25. An ingenious translation of the notion of "works of the law" in Pauline theology.

26. In these Roycean categories one can see paraphrases of the Pauline concept of *kauchāsthai / kaúchēsis / kaúchēma* ("boasting"), used in 1 and 2 Corinthians to describe concrete sin; cf. also Rom. 2:17; 3:27; 4:2.

27. On the origin of the notion of conscience, see Günther Bornkamm, "Gesetz und Natur," in *Studien zu Antike und Urchristentum: Gesammelte Aufsätze, 2,* 3d ed., Beiträge zur Evangelischen Theologie 23 (Munich: Chr. Kaiser, 1970), 93–118, esp. 111–18.

[21]But now the righteousness of God has been manifested apart from law, although the law and the prophets bear witness to it, [22]the righteousness of God through faith in Jesus Christ for all who believe. For there is no distinction; [23]since all have sinned and fall short of the glory of God, [24]they are justified by his grace as a gift, through the redemption which is in Christ Jesus, [25]whom God put forward as an expiation by his blood, to be received by faith. This was to show God's righteousness, because in his divine forbearance he had passed over former sins; [26]it was to prove at the present time that he himself is righteous and that he justifies the one who has faith in Jesus.

He uses a text from the Jesus tradition of Hellenistic Judaism, shaped by the Jewish theology of martyrdom.[28] As 4 Maccabees shows, this theology—with its notion of the beneficial results of the martyrs' heroic death—is quite consonant with Jewish missionary theology. The credal formula cited by Paul amplifies this missionary thrust by extending the benefits of Jesus' death to the Gentiles.[29] The loyalty demonstrated in the witnessing death of Jesus[30] makes it a means of atonement for the Gentiles. They were the very people unaffected by the cult of Israel, whose sins God has passed

28. It is generally accepted that 3:24-26 represents a confession of faith from the early church, but scholars differ as to its extent. Sam K. Williams (*Jesus' Death as Saving Event: The Background and Origin of a Concept,* Harvard Dissertations in Religion [Missoula: Scholars Press, 1975], 5–58) cogently limits it to vv. 25-26a, 26c. He also discusses 4 Maccabees as the background to this credal formula (ibid., 165–202, 233–54). See the discussion above, pp. 68–70.

29. The text used by Paul describes Jesus' death as a means of expiating, indicating that it understands Jesus' death as a martyr's death influencing the course of history, like 4 Maccabees had interpreted the death of the Jewish martyrs.

30. The phrase *pístis Iēsoū* in Rom. 3:26 means the fidelity or loyalty of Jesus (see above, p. 36 n. 10, and p. 84), not his faith in God as Williams, *Jesus' Death as Saving Event,* 5–58, claims. In 3:25, too, the instrumental nature of *pístis* is best explained as a reference to Jesus' fidelity.

over up to now, out of forbearance.[31] The Gentile world would have no difficulty understanding this as a fair and collaborative offer, not least because everyone was convinced of the presence of unwitting and unknown transgressions. Whether one felt impelled to accept the Jewish version of Jesus because one expected personal benefit from it was another question, but a question anyone could understand. This christological tradition made no attempt to criticize religion, the law, or even society. On the contrary, the notion of atonement, which depended on commonly accepted Hellenistic presuppositions,[32] presupposed the general liberal interpretation of the law described above.

There is no reason to assume that the theology of the Jesus community in Rome was anything but such a liberal theology modified to incorporate the figure of Jesus. This theology apparently dominated the missionary work of the primitive church.[33] Paul probably uses the credal formula in 3:24-26 because it was acceptable—and possibly even familiar—to the community to which he was writing. By repeating the word *dikaiosýnē* in his addendum (v. 26b) and integrating the entire quotation into its present context, he reinterprets the text in a way that undoubtedly astonished both its original authors and readers.

31. The Hellenistic world, both Jewish and pagan, would understand *pístis* most of all in the sense of "fidelity" or "loyalty," *díkaios* in the sense of "fair" (characterized by *dikaiosýnē* as *isótēs*), and *dikaioūn* in the sense of "treat fairly." In the light of this usage, I would like to modify Williams's paraphrase of the formula in 3:25-26 (*Jesus' Death as Saving Event*, 34, 50, 54) as follows: "God has treated Jesus as a means of expiation, brought about by Jesus through his loyalty at the price of his own blood. God has done this as a demonstration of his fairness, because he had passed over the former sins [of the Gentiles] out of forbearance. [God did this] that he might [continue to] be fair and treat fairly everyone [characterized] by the loyalty of Jesus."

32. Set forth by Williams, *Jesus' Death as Saving Event*, passim.

33. See, e.g., the miracle stories of the Gospels, many of which have a missionary thrust; the work of Luke; 1 Clement (from Rome!); and the Christian apologists of the second century. Despite their focus on Jesus, at first all of these missionary efforts were pro-Jewish or judaizing; later they became increasingly anti-Jewish.

Undoubtedly Paul understands *dikaiosýnē* to mean more than "fairness." This meaning is included, but in itself is insufficient. The credal formula had already made the nature of God its hidden theme at the end of v. 26. Paul reinforces this tendency in his familiar paradoxical way, especially at the end of v. 23. Here he emphasizes that the entire human race has lost the majesty of God. In the Jesus event, the God of whom Paul is speaking takes common cause with all humanity as a "mass of perdition," the totality described in v. 23. The *dikaiosýnē theoū* manifested in Jesus (3:21) is God's act by which God establishes solidarity with the godless— that is all of humanity.[34]

For Paul, then, God's rulership manifests itself in a unilateral preemptive act. It is an act that by ordinary standards would put at risk if not entirely relinquish rule. The traditional formula declares that the death of Jesus proves his fidelity. Paul underlines his interest in the phrase *pístis Iēsoū* of this tradition by anticipating it in 3:22, albeit restating it as *pístis Christoū*.[35] For Paul, the title "Christ" is the focal point where the dialectical authority of Jesus, crucified and risen, is concentrated. His authority is his loyalty, a loyalty to both God and humanity. More precisely, Jesus is loyal to God's solidarity with sinful humanity. This is Paul's counterpoise to the *theîoi ánthropoi*, the Caesars included. These divine individuals were elevated by death to the status of heroes or even gods and thus removed from the company of the living. As such they reinforced the notion of a divine omnipotence far above the human plane and the concomitant proliferation of such omnipotence—despite a bewildering variety—in contemporary religious and social institutions.

---

34. The argument in Romans 3:21—4:25 shows that for Paul *dikaiosýnē* is an action noun and means the act of establishing solidarity.

35. The added *Iēsoū* of several manuscripts, including Sinaiticus, is an easier reading and therefore secondary.

Sovereignty and Solidarity

In Rom. 5:6-8, Paul gives his interpretation of Jesus' death without reference to any traditional formulas:

> "While we were still weak, at the right time Christ died for the ungodly. [7]Why, one will hardly die for a righteous person—though perhaps for a good person one will dare even to die. [8]But God shows his love for us in that while we were yet sinners Christ died for us."

Here he brings the Christ event more distinctly into the realm of sinners. He describes Jesus' association with all humanity as an association with a company of weak and godless sinners. In the language of sin used by scripture and Rom. 1:18—3:20, Christ associates himself with a company of chaotic anarchists and rebels. He becomes a strange first among equals, a very singular sort of *princeps*. The ruler of the world joins company with those in rebellion against him. This claim defies both Jewish and Roman moral principles, not only as phenomena of individual or religious morality, but as phenomena of social and political ethics and administrative efficiency. Romans 5:6-8 turns martyrdom into a death that establishes solidarity with the rebel and the enemy. This view of martyrdom protests the one-sided understanding of loyalty which prevailed in contemporary social and political life. There, loyalty means first and foremost the loyalty of subjects to their rulers. Paul declares an end to the deadly cycle of power, privilege, law, justice, and violence.

The unilateral preemptive act of Christ brings about the deliverance of all human beings—not only from sin, but also from the law and the alienation and corruption[36] brought about by the law.[37] The death of Jesus establishes solidarity between

36. Compare Rom. 3:21 with 1:18—3:20, and 5:6-8 with 5:20-21.
37. Including Jewish and Roman law, which supposedly represent law in its "liberal" and "humane" form.

humanity and God. Yet in 3:27 Paul can speak of the law in positive terms, as the bar to any kind of privilege.[38] Paul asks: what law really reflects the demand that law should bar all kinds of privilege? He answers: not a law concerned with works,[39] which promotes achievement; but the law that is concerned with *pístis*, the loyalty of Christ (described above), the confidence displayed by Christ in his active engagement with the human condition. Hellenistic civilization aspired to an ideal of justice that it failed to realize and instead perverted. The confidence of Christ makes this ideal reality. Christ does not demand renunciation of privilege but bestows and realizes privilege by giving himself freely.[40] Romans 3:31 makes it absolutely clear that in 3:27-31 Paul identifies God's law and God's fidelity: God's loyalty is God's law; establishment of solidarity with humanity is God's sovereignty.

Romans 5:12-21 explicates Phil. 2:6-11, Galatians 3, and 1 Corinthians 12. It presents Jesus as the one who through his obedience became the embodiment of a new and authentic humanity. In this new humanity justice means participatory solidarity and therein signifies the sovereignty of all (5:17). This sovereignty is not in obedience to the will expressed in law but in obedience to the creaturely limitations of human existence, vulnerability, and weakness.[41]

---

38. Hellenistic thought, notably since Aristotle, emphasized even more than biblical thought that the law treats all people the same and renders them equal. Roman law in particular addressed all without distinction, both subjects and rulers. Roman jurisprudence required *aequitas*, that is, identical verdicts in identical cases.

39. The genitive in *nómos érgōn* ("law of works"), as well as in the following phrase *nómos písteōs* ("law of loyalty"), is explicative.

40. Romans 3:28 does not speak about human faith but about the loyalty of God and of Jesus, which irresistibly and irreversibly establishes solidarity with humanity. Romans 3:29 radicalizes the Jewish affirmation that God is one: the God who is one is the God of all. That is why in the future, too, God will declare God's solidarity with all, including the Gentiles. This is also the argument of Romans 4.

41. Romans 1:5 and Romans 5 undertake a revision of the concept of obedience, an attitude in which the Romans were well versed. Romans 6 develops this revision further: obedience is not an appropriate subordination to the superior authority of rulers and judges but a responsible reaction to demonstrated solidarity in the surrender of privileges, rights, and power (see esp. vv. 13, 22). Obedience is thus not a one-way road to subjection but a confident response to demonstrated loyalty and solidarity.

In Rom. 5:6-11 and 15-21, Paul competes with Augustus and his successors. They were, allegedly, the first among equals, and according to their propaganda, representatives of a new kind of human being. Paul, however, makes Jesus of Nazareth, who accepts death, represent the new humanity. Moreover, Jesus signifies the new world of reconciliation and peace—not as a model of hegemony or authority, but as an exemplar of partnership. He is not a paradigm of the force bound to death, but rather the prototype of a community pledged to life.[42]

Romans 5, to be sure, also uses Jewish ideas (Adam/ Christ, etc.). But they have been permeated by Jewish Gnosticism[43] and are intended to compete in a critical fashion with the notions of a new age (*saeculum*) which have been embodied in a single individual, the Caesar. This idea flourished once again during the period of the principate. Romans was written at the very beginning of Nero's rule, when propaganda based on such prophetic and theological speculations, with intense eschatological expectations, enjoyed great popularity.[44] For Paul, Jesus is what the *princeps* claimed to be: representative of humanity, reconciler and ruler of the world. Jesus is all this because he demonstrates the association and identification of God with those in rebellion against

42. The *Pax Romana* is based on the theory of an eternal Rome, whose foremost representatives are divine and immortal, as well as on the power of the Roman army and Roman money. The result—not only in the view of the rulers—was deliverance from foreign domination and internecine warfare, self-determination, and the freedom to form coalitions with others in a world civilization and world economy that people thought they could enjoy freely but that in fact enslaved them to the principle of achievement and the constraint of possessions. The *Pax Christi* is based on acceptance of human existence with all its limitations and mutual interdependence. *Pax Christi* means the freedom and the surrender of all privileges by everyone. This renunciation of privilege, according to Romans 5, is the true authority which moves and shapes the world.

43. See Egon Brandenburger, *Adam und Christus: Exegetisch-religionsgeschichtliche Untersuchungen zu Römer 5, 12-21 (1.Kor. 15)*, Wissenschaftliche Monographien zum Alten und Neuen Testament 7 (Neukirchen: Neukirchener Verlag, 1968), passim.

44. See the Neronian Eclogues of the Einsiedeln Papyrus as well as the first, fourth, and seventh eclogues of Titus Calpurnius Piso.

God. He represents the weakness of God and thus the dominion of grace, the sole form of dominion befitting both humanity and God. The return of the golden age expected under Nero comes face to face with a humanity whose solidarity is established by Jesus.

It has become commonplace to look upon personal affirmation of faith and affiliation with ecclesial institutions as conditions for receiving the righteousness and reconciliation of Jesus. Romans 5 flatly contradicts any such mindset. Solidarity (righteousness, justice), reconciliation, and peace are *givens*, and they are for *everyone*. They are the reality of Jesus, which applies to the whole world. Here Paul leaves Roman ideas about peace far behind. Despite all the talk about one world united in peace, these ideas are still based on social and geographical boundaries, on superiority and inferiority. They have, in other words, conditions and prerequisites for admission.

In Rom. 8:2, as in 3:27 and 3:31, Paul speaks of the law in positive terms. In the latter he speaks of the law of *pístis*. Here he speaks about the law of the spirit. The hortatory section of Romans (chapters 12–15), like the exhortations of the other Pauline letters, arises from this spiritual law, the law of Christ of Gal. 6:2. This law is not a demand, a norm, or an authority. It is, rather, an environment of loyalty and solidarity, of fidelity and confidence, of spirit and community. Thus the law becomes a prophetic entity, an expression of creative power and imagination. It establishes neither the past nor the present, binding and limiting the future. It opens the future and is a message of freedom.

Chapter 8 speaks of creative freedom in spiritual community, a community that transcends all hard and fast boundaries. This community includes the natural world. For Paul, nature and humanity share a common fate (8:12-30, esp. vv. 18-25). This idea distinguishes Pauline theology sharply from the political theology of Rome. There, nature plays an important role, but it is discussed in idyllic terms.[45] Paul speaks

---

45. Typical are the eclogues from Vergil to Piso, but see also the *Carmen saeculare*

instead of how all creation, including the physical world, groans under the corruption brought about by the collaboration between humanity and the law.[46] For Paul, the difference between humanity and nature is the fact that the latter will come to share in the freedom of creation only in the future, when it is delivered from all the consequences of human depravity. The eschatological freedom envisioned in 8:12-30 is freedom from all dominion, freedom to be children.[47]

The end of the law in the reality of Jesus (10:4) means not only the end of norms but also the end of normative and authoritarian (allegedly protective) power. It also signals the end of the prestige that accompanies this power including the prestige of God.[48] Salvation is opposed to power and authority. The Roman theology of peace, on the other hand, is intimately associated with the restoration of legal authority and power. It promises the revival of institutional and cultic prestige, along with the revival of *auctoritas* (sovereignty). These are the principles that establish and uphold society. In Romans 12, however (recalling and elaborating the image of the body which he applied in 1 Corinthians 12), Paul enlists the idea of peace he has been developing throughout Romans to call for a democratized worship closely tied to everyday life.[49] Such worship is not exalted above the ordinary workaday realm like the cream of society. Rather it goes much further: Romans 12 maintains that worship is ethics and that recognition of ethical responsibility is worship. But ethics is not the dictation and regulation of life. It is not a body of commandments and prohibitions, either individual or collective.

---

and the odes and epodes of Horace; see Georgi, "Who Is the True Prophet?" in *Christians Among Jews and Gentiles;* George W. Nickelsberg, George W. MacRae (Philadelphia: Fortress Press, 1986), 102–21.

46. Romans 8:18-22, retrospectively summarizing Rom. 1:18—3:20 and 7:7-24.

47. Verses 14-17 and 26-30 provide the essential context for vv. 18-25 and describe proleptically the nature of this eschatological freedom: the freedom to be vulnerable.

48. This is the theme of Romans 9, which speaks of God in terms of despotic capriciousness.

49. See Ernst Käsemann, "Gottesdienst im Alltag der Welt," *Exegetische Versuche und Besinnungen*, 6th ed. (Göttingen: Vandenhoeck & Ruprecht, 1975), 2:189–203.

True ethics means charismatic responsibility in communal interchange and dialogue based on love, that is, in participation inspired by the Spirit.

Paul's treatment of the relationship of Christians to the political and legal authorities is an example of his critical imagination. The period was one of increasing political centralization, and there was a great emphasis on the ideology of Caesar's authority and power. Yet Paul, in this letter to the citizens of the capital, never mentions the *princeps* or the special status of Rome. And in Rom. 13:1-7, he borrows a fragment of Jewish tradition from the republican period. By citing this anachronistic tradition (particularly during this time of increasing centralization), Paul gives the passage a critical slant: he urges decentralization and undermines the ideology that supports the majesty of the state. The summation and interpretation of Rom. 13:1-7 in 13:8-14 makes it clear that political ethics cannot be separated from the ethics of love. The later (largely post-Constantinian) distinction between secular and spiritual, visible and invisible, private and civic, shatters Paul's goal of solidarity and unification. For Paul, eschatology belongs to the present world and the separation of ethics is abrogated. Not just Romans 12–13 (a distinct unit) but the entire letter demands the inclusion of politics in the spiritual realm—never its exclusion.[50]

Romans 14, moreover, gives practical examples for the realization of the solidarity of God in the workaday world. This solidarity appears as a continuous reconciliation between ideological divisions as they manifest themselves in praxis. Paul sees the congregation as pluralistic model-society.

The universality of Paul's vision stands in the foreground once again in Rom. 15:7ff., an undisguised echo of the popular picture of Alexander. Romans 15:3, 5, 7-8 depicts Jesus once

---

50. I have discussed Rom. 13:1-7 in n. 40 of the exegetical notes on the "Theologische Auseinandersetzung mit den Einwänden gegen die Thesen der Bruderschaften" of the Badische Theologische Sozietät in Ernst Wolf, ed., *Christusbekenntnis im Atomzeitalter?* Theologische Existenz heute 70 (Munich: Chr. Kaiser, 1959), 130–31.

more as the archetype of solidarity, overcoming all distinctions of class and system. From Jesus' solidarity with the Jews, Paul deduces the solidarity of Jews and Gentiles. Paul's own mission is a sign of this universal solidarity (15:14-33). His journey to Jerusalem and delivery of the collection are also instruments of this solidarity. Paul's mission continues and fulfills the mission of Jesus (prematurely interrupted, like that of Alexander). Paul's activity signifies the mission of all the witnesses to Jesus (see also 15:4-6). By completing the unfinished work of Alexander with the help of Jesus' followers in the capital of the world, the Pauline engagement serves the entire human race, including the peoples of the western regions of the Mediterranean, which Alexander never reached.

No exegesis of Romans can ignore the fact that its author was almost certainly a prisoner when he came to Rome, the city where he was to be tried and executed. On the indirect evidence of Acts 28:30-31 and 1 Clement 5, both Paul and Peter were charged and convicted independently of (and probably before) the persecution ordered by Nero. There is no reason to believe that the Jewish charges of desecrating the temple in Jerusalem could have endangered Paul before an imperial court in Rome. A normal criminal charge is out of the question, as is a charge of *superstitio*.[51] The eloquent apologetic silence of Luke, friend to both Paul and the Romans, suggests a different explanation: the *crimen (laesae) maiestatis*, or treason. The argument employed by Paul in Romans, especially if its protective code is cracked, could easily lead to such a trial and justify a negative verdict. The difference between Paul's arraignment and the later persecutions (and convictions) of the Christians would be that

51. See, e.g., the charges in the Bacchanalia trial of 186 B.C.E. (Livy *Ab urbe condita* 9.2–19.2); see Dieter Georgi, "Analyse des Liviusberichts über den Bacchanalienskandal," in *Unterwegs für die Volkskirche,* FS Dieter Stoodt, ed. Wilhelm-Ludwig Federlin and Edmund Weber (Frankfurt/Main: Lang, 1987), 191–207. Under such circumstances, the judiciary and the police would certainly have investigated the entire Christian community, at least in Rome. There is no trace of such an investigatit even during the persecution of 64 C.E.

Paul's crime was not passive resistance (refusal to sacrifice to the emperor). Rather, it was an active one, an act of political aggression. This explanation would account well for the apologetic smoke-screen laid down by Luke and the Pastorals (and by the later ecclesiastical tradition). 1 Clement already exhibits this tendency, albeit not so clearly as Luke or the Pastorals. Still, it is noteworthy that 1 Clem. 5:7 uses the phrase *dikaiosýnēn didáxas* ("having taught righteousness") to describe Paul's preaching which led to his martyrdom, thereby echoing the theme of Romans. When Luke turned Paul into a religious hero, the fool for Christ was given a belated state funeral. When the victorious wing of the church allied itself with the Caesar, Paul, the rebel for Christ whom Caesar had slain was consigned to a golden hell. Since that day, has up been up and down been down? Can the gods once again dwell in peace in heaven and rulers stand secure once more upon the backs of their subjects?

INDEX

Hebrew Bible

New Testament

Jewish Literature
Apocrypha

Pseudepigrapha

Nag Hammadi Texts

Greek and Latin Authors

De vita Mosis
  1.148-59, 212-13   *44 n.35*
  2.7, 46-47, 188-92, 288-91   *44 n.35*
Leg. All.
  3.217   *43 n.33*
Legatio ad Gaium
  143–153   *15 n.34*

Plato
  Symposium
    179B   *68 n.90*
  Timaeus
    32C-33A   *34 n.1*

Plutarch
  De Alexandri Magni fortuna
    329-30   *65-66*
  De communibus notitiis
    1076   *75 n.102*
  De Iside et Osiride
    316E, 364F, 365A   *70 n.96*

Seneca
  Apocolocynthosis 86

Sibylline Oracles
  3.782   *13 n.26*
  3.787   *13 n.25*

Strabo
  80   n.1

Titus Calpurnius Piso
  Eclogues
    1, 4, 7   *99 n.44*

Vergil
  Aen.
    5.814-16   *69 n.94*

Early Christian Literature

Clement of Rome
  1 Clement
  — *95 n.33*
  5 *103-104*

Modern Authors

Arthur, R. H., 12 n.20, 41 n.24, 46 n.38

Beker, J. C., 7 n.8
Bertram, G., 34 n.6, 38 n.14
Best, E., 26 n.21
Betz, H. D., 18 n.3, 19 n.3, 38 n.13, 42 n.26, 64 n.82
Bodin, J., viii-x, viii n.2
Bornkamm, G., 61 n.75, 80 n.2, 82 n.4, 89 n.19, 93 n.27
Brandenburger, E., 59 n.72, 67 n.88, 99 n.43
Brinsmead, B., 35 n.7
Bultmann, R., 19 n.7, 90 n.21, 92, 92 n.24

Campenhausen, H. von, 49 n.51, 56 n.66
Collins, A. Y., 43 n.33
Colson, F. H., 14 n.31
Conzelmann, H., 28 n.26, 52 n.62, 76 n.106
Cross, F. M., 2 n.1, 23 n.20

Dahl, N.A., 10 n.16
Dewey, A., 37 n.11, 39 n.16, 40, 40 nn.18-22; 42 n.30, 43 n.31
Dibelius, M., 26 n.23, 28 n.26, 56 n.66
Dittenberger, W., 48 n.50, 83 n.5
Dupont, J., 26 n.21

Eisenhut, W., 84 n.6

Fallon, F. T., 44 n.34, 45 nn.36, 37
Fiorenza, E. S., 63 n.78
Förster, E., 30 n.31
Fuchs, E., 92 n.24

Gelzer, T., 50 n.58
Georgi, D., x n.4, 3 n.2, 6 n.6, 7 nn.7, 9; 11 n.18, 12 nn.21-23; 13 n.24, 15 n.36, 17 n.1, 22 n.13, 23 n.19, 29 n.30, 42 n.26, 50 n.56, 56 n.68, 61 n.75, 62 n.77; 63 n.78, 64 nn.82, 84; 67 n.87, 68 n.89, 72 n.99, 78 n.109, 80 n.1, 81 n.3, 86 n.14, 100 n.45,

Greek and Latin Words (Selective)

Subject